D1644040

UNBOUND

UNBOUND
The Transformative Power of Youth Mission Trips

COVER DESIGN: Elizabeth Fenimore
INTERIOR DESIGN: Marti Naughton

PUBLISHER: Huff Publishing Associates, LLC
ISBN: 978-0-9910600-0-9

UNBOUND

THE TRANSFORMATIVE POWER OF YOUTH MISSION TRIPS

by JANN TREADWELL

Retired Certified Christian Educator
2010 Educator of the Year for the Association of Presbyterian Church Educators

To my husband—John—for his constant encouragement, love and support.

To my most consistent partners in crime—Wayne, Gary, and Grant who accompanied me on 10, 12, and 11 trips respectively—for the laughter, memories, and hard work.

CONTENTS

INTRODUCTION

There is a picture, a collage of pictures actually, that is framed and sits on my desk. It has followed me through the latter half of my seminary education, and into three separate calls as minister of Word and Sacrament in the Presbyterian Church, USA. It depicts a mission trip to Farrell-Sherard, Mississippi in June of 1997. Here a group of wonderful youth participants and adult volunteers taught a wet-behind-the ears seminary intern much of the ministry of Jesus Christ. Here a wonderful Director of Christian Education quietly guided this intern through the hazy and often intense back streets of ministering to youth.

While this mission trip was only one of many memorable experiences at NorthPark Presbyterian Church, it stands out because it was there that I felt most intensely God's call to channel my thirst for theology and Biblical studies into the parish. It was here that my heart for ministry found resonance with God's providence, as these youth and staff confirmed to me what I had yet to fully realize, that my call to ministry was to be fulfilled in the parish. While our task that summer was to build a house, for me, this trip built a future.

REV. BRENT HAMPTON, 1997 seminary intern at NorthPark Presbyterian Church

It was nearly impossible to go on a Mission Trip and not have the importance of our call to serve others slap us in the face. To see the struggles of others was eye opening and moving. To see the smiles of those we were serving was always an incredible

feeling. I remember thinking so many times how truly easy it was to make someone smile. Nothing we were doing on the job sites was all that complex. Sometimes we served by paying attention to another person. A ball or frisbee and whatever game we came up with was all it took to make a kid's day.

Mission trips simplified for me who God calls us to be. We knew we were called to be servants but it was these trips that taught us how easy it was to be a servant. We left these trips with a renewed sense of hope for the world and better understandings of just how simple it can be to be a servant every day. One person could make a huge difference in the life of another. It is my belief that our Mission Trips impacted our lives in ways that made us all understand the call to serve as well as the intangible rewards received from serving.

Fast forward twenty years and take a look at what some of the people who went on these trips have chosen as careers. They have become pastors, nurses, people working for non-profit agencies, soldiers, chefs, police officers, teachers, and several other career paths that focus on serving others. And so many of us are still involved in the Church. This result was no accident.

SETH: five youth and college trips from 1995 to 2003; adult sponsor in 2004

Mission trips are a powerful way to nurture the faith of youth and adults. Having organized twenty-nine of them over twenty-two years, my understanding of, and witness to, their power has grown and become my passion. Other Christian educators and lay people have discovered the same thing. Though I certainly do not claim that the particular trips that I set up are the "be all and end all," I hope that readers will find in this little book helpful information and inspiration to organize their first trips or find new ideas for their next trip. As a Presbyterian-type Christian, my thoughts and planning are steeped in my understanding of the Reformed tradition. That said, I hope anyone connected to any faith-based organization will find the information helpful, whether you are a lay mission trip leader, youth sponsor, parent, educator, or pastor who desires to execute such a trip.

Over the years the format of the trips has evolved as my own faith has expanded. On the early trips I was still feeling my way into the world of adolescent ministry and was far too hesitant to "impose" any type of extended Bible study or spiritual discussion for fear of turning the youth off. We played a lot of games in the evenings rather than nurture the spiritual hunger that I later realized was deep inside them and that had grown inside me as well. The practical aspects of the trips, from entrusting the youth with meals and cleanup and dealing with conflict, also changed as my awareness grew of young people's need to be responsible partners with the adults. These experiences opened my eyes to new ways of sharpening the focus of our acts of discipleship so that they would better reflect Christ's love and service. God has used my careless oversights and occasional moments of disorganization, as well as my moments of inspiration and tendency to plan ahead, to help form these trips into what have been life-giving and life-changing experiences for the participants, as you will see from their comments. They have been so for me too.

Not only do I offer details and practical ways to put together such trips (accompanied by suggested "to do" lists), I have included stories and reflections from the youth and adults who have been on these journeys with me over the years. Their thoughts confirm the power of service opportunities.

The support of the pastors, staff, and congregations of two Dallas churches, Ridgeview Presbyterian Church and NorthPark Presbyterian Church, made these twenty-nine trips possible. The youth and sponsors who brought energy and commitment made the trips profound. Christ gave the trips purpose and passion. It is with a grateful heart that I offer this book to God's glory.

1

Why Do a
MISSION TRIP?

In the Reformed tradition, the simple reason for why we do mission trips is that we are saved in order to serve. But, you say, we can serve in our own back yards. Need is everywhere and it is constant. Why pile kids and sponsors into a van and drive for hours to a far-off place?

There are three reasons:

Theological. God calls us to do so.

Developmental. Mission trips build a youth faith community.

Practical. Mission trips teach us valuable life lessons.

THEOLOGICAL REASONS FOR MISSION TRIPS

The trips allowed me to add action to my faith, and to see action in others' faith. The best way to follow Jesus is not just to read about him all the time, but to follow how he acted, to be a blessing to the people around you.

The other thing I want to emphasize was the simplicity of the trips. Our destination was always a van ride, not a plane ride, away. We made our own meals and ate them together. We only went out to eat once or twice per trip. We stayed in places where some had to sleep on the floor. The work was not groundbreaking, it was simple: providing a home for someone who needs one. I truly believe that is what much of Jesus' life looked like: simple. He came to show the people of the world that he loved them, and he did that by spending time with them. He and his disciples walked together through

*everything, and that was the spirit of our trips. We do these
things together.*

ROBBIE: three high school and two college trips from 2005-2010

Scripture is filled with mandates to serve and to reach out to those
in need. Among the most familiar stories about Jesus is the one in John
13 in which he washes the disciples' feet and the Matthew 25 passage
about offering someone thirsty a cup of cold water, clothing the naked,
and feeding the hungry. That said, the biblical image that has affected me
most personally and has become my vision for ministry is the story of
the raising of Lazarus. In John 11:44, when Lazarus came out of the tomb
wrapped in grave cloths, Jesus said to the people, "Unbind him and let
him go." This is what all disciples are called to do. We are chosen to live
in relationship with God and with others and to unbind one another from
our biases, feelings of inadequacy, or lack of knowledge and experience.

Mission trips offer rich opportunities for us to unbind one another
and to be unbound by others. We go out to serve those in need, helping
in a community that is bound up by poverty, lack of education, and job
opportunities, hoping to unbind someone with a new home and a sense
of dignity, and offering friendship and affirmation. In my experience we
have never left without realizing that the recipients have unbound us as
well. They have unwrapped us from our grave cloths of complacency
and prejudice, of limited tolerance and of pigeon-holing the poor. They
have given us gifts that far outweigh what we have given them. Mutual
unbinding is biblical.

As we live into this call as baptized people of God, we are part of
God's bigger story. We read of others who were called by God to carry out
God's purposes: in Exodus 3:4, for example, God called Moses from out
of a burning bush. After Moses said, "Here I am," God instructed him to
deliver the Hebrews from slavery. The prophet Isaiah heard God speak
(Isaiah 6:8-9), answered with "Here am I; send me," and responded to God's
command to speak hard words to the Hebrews about their unfaithfulness.
Each of the gospels relates the story of Jesus calling his disciples to follow
him. As part of God's family, we, too, are responsible to listen and act.

In his classic book, *Christian Doctrine,* Shirley Guthrie offers these
thoughts on what it means to be the chosen people of God: "We too are
chosen not *instead of* but *for the sake of* the world's outsiders. We are chosen
not to *escape from* a godless and godforsaken world with all its sinfulness
and suffering, but to be *sent into it* and *live for it.* We are chosen not so

we can congratulate ourselves because we live in the light while everyone else gropes in the darkness, but to be a light that shines in their darkness. We are chosen so that those who are excluded from the benefits of God's loving justice and just love may be included. For we too are chosen not to be served but to serve."[1]

WE SERVE BECAUSE WE MUST
AS CHRIST'S DISCIPLES.

DEVELOPMENTAL REASONS FOR MISSION TRIPS

The mission trip was one of the highlights of my years in high school and college. Each year, I made new friends, reconnected with old friends, laughed, cried, sang, played, and worked hard. The trips instilled in me a spirit of service and giving that has followed me through my whole life. It is through service to others that we ourselves become truly whole.

KARA: four high school and two college trips from 1996-2004; adult sponsor 2007

Young people need to belong. They need to feel accepted by others. They need adults in addition to their parents who will listen and be supportive, and they need to be involved in something significant. A mission trip addresses these needs.

Belonging is a huge deal in the adolescent world. Forming cliques and bending to peer pressure are evidence of the deep yearning to be a part of a group. At a youth conference years ago I learned that it takes at least fifteen hours to build community. A six-day mission trip offers plenty of time for bonds to form, even among the most unlikely, as shared experiences cement friendships. Living together in a different setting for several days can build community in a way little else can.

Intentionally placing youth on work teams with those they do not know well diffuses the issue of cliques and strengthens a sense of belonging and purpose. Adult sponsors play a vital role in this process. Chapter 2 says more about this adult role.

Adolescence is a formative time in which values are solidified, and the mission trip offers a phenomenal opportunity to plant the seeds of a life of service. According to generational theory, the current American youth are "Millennials," born between 1982 and 2002. They are part of the next civic generation, a generation that seems to be more open to the concept of service and community than the previous two generations.[2] Mission trips can nurture this innate awareness of the needs of others and the desire to give of oneself to the larger good, helping youth to develop further the altruistic nature that is characteristic of many in this age group. As the authors of generational theory have observed, "A new Millennial service ethic is emerging, built around notions of collegial (rather than individual) action, support for (rather than resistance against) civic institutions, and the tangible doing of good deeds." [3]

This "tangible doing of good deeds" gives a sense of accomplishment as youth realize they are more than capable of responding to those in need. Observing, in person, the plight of other individuals and communities helps the youth to discover that parts of our cultural patterns of living can be oppressive. This awareness prompts a desire to find solutions and continue selfless efforts on behalf of others.

A significant lesson on these trips for all of us is our growing awareness of the many ways in which we are a global community, interdependent, and working in partnership with those we came to serve. We always return home having been inspired by the recipients who offered us a new vision of hospitality as they embraced us, showed generosity by sharing their time and food with us, and gave a powerful witness to us through their open faith.

> *We came away (from our two trips) with a bunch of thoughts: to appreciate what we had, to know that giving back was our responsibility, and that God's love was alive and well in the hearts of folks that have it so very hard. They didn't blame, they didn't hate, they didn't demand; they opened their arms and hearts to us and showed us what being a Christian was truly all about.*
>
> SUSAN and ROCKY: adult sponsors on my first two trips, 1988, 1989

WE SERVE BECAUSE WE MUST
AS HUMANS LIVING
IN A WORLD WITH NEEDS.

PRACTICAL REASONS FOR MISSION TRIPS

I often wonder if these groups we are helping might be better off if we mailed them the money instead of using that money to transport our group of "highly unskilled" labor to them. But the beauty of the gig is not the money, but in the life experience of those people that go on the trip, it's in the cultural exchanges happening when we get face to face with the people we've come to help.

GARY: adult sponsor of twelve trips, 1999-2010

Shouldn't mission work be done locally? There's so much need here at home.

Of course, and that is important and necessary. Should funding be spent to travel away from home? Indeed it should, if possible. Larger cities such as Dallas have resources to meet some of the needs of many who are living in poverty, but there are areas of the country where resources are slim to none.

In addition, living among those who are less advantaged broadens the world view of the youth which is often limited to school, family, and a circle of friends whose problems and challenges are similar to their own. Getting away from home for several days raises in them an awareness of the struggles of others that they cannot gain from working on a local service project in the daytime, then going home to air conditioning, TV, and pizza that evening. To live among those in need, even for a few days, sometimes without air conditioning or other conveniences, gives youth and adults a greater sensitivity to others. Without the comforts of home, there are no easy distractions, and this allows new perspectives to develop.

All of us learn best through direct, personal experience. Praxis is in play on mission trips through the acts of "doing" and then reflecting on where God is in the "doing." This contributes to faith maturity, as do the experiences that bump up against our understanding of where and how God is at work.

The practical skills learned on mission trips build self-confidence. To master a challenging task, to be entrusted with a responsibility to complete an assignment, or to know that the results of our efforts will provide someone else with a home for the first time: each contributes to a sense of self-worth. While most of our youth will not become dry-wall professionals, or painters, or rough carpenters, doing work that is significant and meaningful for another brings a feeling of accomplishment not often available to young people.

The daily give-and-take forced upon us through community-living circumstances such as sharing chores, bathrooms, and showers offers opportunities for personal growth. When the group has to arise in assigned shifts, always earlier than desired, in order to utilize the limited bathroom space and get to the worksite on time, the needs of the group take priority over the desires of individuals. Group decisions on how to spend a free afternoon mean that each person will not get their first choice of activity. The realities of group living shift the focus from the self to the community forcing us to see the perspectives of others.

Youth look forward to the next mission trip all year. This anticipation brings with it a sense of excitement that the older ones share with the younger youth who are looking forward to their own involvement. They share with one another stories of the joys of serving. They feel pride in representing the mission of their own home church, perhaps for the first time in their lives.

> *These mission trips have allowed me to realize the importance of helping others. It is because of my experiences on these trips that I actively participate in community service today and become excited about opportunities to help others. I look forward to them every summer because it is a week away from home in which I get to make a difference in someone's life and also have fun with some of my favorite people. Working with and living with your youth group for a week builds a very strong sense of community that remains in your heart even after you return home.*

SEAN: three high school trips, 2008-2010

WE SERVE BECAUSE WE HAVE
BEEN GIVEN MUCH AND ARE REQUIRED
TO SHARE WITH THOSE WHO ARE
LESS ADVANTAGED.

1. Shirley C. Guthrie, *Christian Doctrine* (Westminster/John Knox Press, 1994), 140.

2. William Strauss and Neil Howe, *Generations: The History of America's Future, 1584 to 2069* (Harper Collins Publishers, 1991), 335-43.

3. Neil Howe and William Strauss, *Millennials Rising: The Net Great Generation* (Vintage Books, 2000), 216.

2

⎯⎯⎯⎯⎯⎯⎯⎯⎯⎯⎯

RELATIONSHIPS & COMMUNITY:
Pivotal Factors in Unbinding

Many factors contribute to an atmosphere that encourages our unbinding of others and that lowers our resistance to being unbound. At our church, we place a high priority on creating a comfort level within the group through strengthening relationships and building community. Community building is an ongoing endeavor throughout the year, but intentional efforts also need to be made during the trip. Feeling like a part of the group helps us to remove barriers that hinder the movement of God's Spirit and the connection between what we do and what we profess. In addition, our Reformed belief in the priesthood of all believers means that each participant has something to offer in the unbinding process. For we know with certainty that God's Spirit is at work in every person, whether a youth, an adult sponsor, or someone from the community to which we have traveled to do ministry together.

RELATIONSHIPS WITH ADULT SPONSORS

The role of sponsors as encouraging mentors and adult friends is crucial to the adventure and pivotal to community building. Sponsors make sure that everyone is included in the work, play, and worship experiences. These special adults are hand-chosen for their ability to relate to youth, to be good listeners and friends who have no ego-based agenda of their own. They are to be solid role models for the teens as they work side-by-side. The sponsors help clarify faith issues for all participants whether during an informal card game or the nightly Bible study.

Doing mission trips demonstrated to me in a direct way how important it is for teens to have trusted adults—other than their parents—take an interest in them. The youth are interesting young adults. Insightful, sensitive, earnest, sometimes profound, and always funny. I have seldom laughed as much as during a week of mission trip!

I always felt that it was my privilege to go on these trips with the youth, to get to know them, to gain their trust, and to participate in their sharing. In the nightly devotion and sharing sessions, and just as important, in the informal interactions that occurred during leisure time and meals, youth open up. Hearing them pour out their hearts, with their fears, hope, and dreams, I often marveled about how valuable it would be for their parents to hear them talk like this. And believe me, you would hear everything. This was particularly poignant with youth living in broken homes, as they would describe their sadness and frustrations with dealing, for instance, with absent fathers.

GARY: adult sponsor of twelve trips, 1999-2010

As Gary said, the youth are insightful. They know what's going on.

In some programs, chaperones sit together at dinner, sit in the front of the van, work together on the job site, spending more time together as chaperones than with us, the kids, but on the NorthPark trips it wasn't about them. The adults came to spend time with us, to eat with us, to hang out for twelve hours in the van with us, to work alongside us, to play Spades with us, to invest in us. I am sure there were times when it was awkward, and maybe they felt weird sitting hanging out with kids ten to thirty-plus years younger than them, but looking back I see [their interaction with kids] as such a strong presentation of the gospel. Jesus consistently put himself in uncomfortable situations around people he was ridiculed for being around, and I do not think it is too much of a stretch of imagination to parallel that with what the youth sponsors were doing.

ROBBIE: three high school and two college trips, 2006-2010

I think one of the good things about mission trips was getting to see others in your group, students and leaders, outside of their shell. Anyone can show their best for an hour during Sunday School or youth group, but spend a week with them and you get to know who they really are. You see the type of people your leaders are 24/7 and it lets you know you can be that type of person, too.

MIKE: two high school trips, 1988 and 1990

After a long day of work, adults and youth were often physically exhausted. As exhausted as we were, it now amazes me how we were able to stay awake into the late hours of the night. It was at these late hours that some of my best conversations with adults and youth occurred. I can think of several trips and several occasions when a small group of us would stay awake discussing the deep topics. We talked about why bad things happened to good people. We talked about Baptism and what it means in our faith. And of course we talked about girlfriends and boyfriends among many other topics.

What made these conversations so special was that normally there was one of our adult leaders participating. They listened to our thoughts and struggles as we shared them, and often shared their own without dominating the conversation. They were there to comfort those who needed comfort and quietly laugh with those who needed to laugh. As a youth it was so cool to be able to share our true thoughts and feelings in the presence of our adult sponsors. These were the adults who I thought would have the answers to our faith and life questions. I'm not sure if they ever truly knew how much weight their words held. I would say the relationships with the sponsors meant the most and had the most impact on my life as a youth, but the words they spoke in these late night conversations had a great impact as well.

SETH: four high school and one college trip, 1995-2003; adult sponsor in 2004

It is helpful to have sponsors who are grounded in their faith. Teachable moments pop up constantly on these trips:

> *I remember working on a house in Mississippi that unfortunately was located next to the neighborhood watering hole or "juke joint." It was hot and while we were working, the establishment began to fill up with a lot of, presumably, able-bodied men. They sat on the front porch with their beverages, watching us work. One of the teenagers came to me and said, "You mean we are taking our vacation to work in this heat for somebody we don't even know, and these so-called neighbors are just gonna sit there and drink and watch?" I said, "What a perfect example of the good Samaritan."*
>
> WAYNE: adult sponsor on ten mission trips

On a different note, most of us are aware of the pitfalls of adult/teen relationships, so guidelines for the adults need to be clear. NorthPark has a Child Protection Policy requiring all adults who work with those under eighteen to submit to a criminal background check. If your church does not have a Child Protection Policy, I would urge you to create one. Resources and suggestions for creating such a policy might be found on your denominational website. For the PCUSA, these resources can be found at www.pcusa.org/sexualmisconduct. In addition, other precautions are taken while on these trips:

- Respect a teen's personal space. We are a "hugging" church, which is a great sign of greeting, but we must realize that some youth are not comfortable with that. Ask their permission for a hug. Make sure there is no touching that a youth might consider inappropriate.

- Some of the most significant moments in youth ministry happen one-on-one between teen and adult, so it is recommended that if a teen wants to talk privately with you that you inform another adult where you will be going and about how long you plan to be gone.

- If you are staying at a motel or cabin, leave the door open when anyone of the opposite sex is in the room.

LIVING IN COMMUNITY HOLDS CHALLENGES AS WELL AS FUN

My strongest impression when I think back on our mission trips as a whole is one of family. For example, when Jenny, Mary, and I got sick in Mexico, much of the group (some whom I barely knew at the time) rallied together to care for us and get us safely home. In Taos, when we had some "high school drama" happening within the group, we all sat down for a discussion and pretty much immediately squashed it. I think it is this trip where I decided to follow a personal philosophy of: don't say anything about someone behind their back that you aren't prepared to say to their face. It has served me well.

Our Mississippi trips in particular hold memories of staying up way too late in the common room coloring on a poster, putting together jigsaw puzzles, playing Spades, talking, and a lot of times just acting ridiculous. And, all of this doesn't even mention the long, hot, but exceedingly rewarding days we spent working with each other on the houses. We would get tired and frustrated and sometimes take it out on each other, but at the end of the day, we'd all come back together. These are not experiences of a disparate group, but those of a family—and a well-adjusted one at that! I think there is something about working towards a common goal, particularly a selfless one, that lends itself to a kind of unity, but I like to think that our group was pretty special.

CYNTHIA: six high school and college trips, 1997-2002

CONFLICT IS INEVITABLE

Conflicts will arise within the group at some point or points on the trip. My modus operandi is to handle discord sooner rather than later as the situation can only get worse by ignoring it. If the conflict involves two or three individuals, I have met with them away from the group and brought the issues into the open. This gives everyone a chance to release feelings, express themselves and work out a solution, or at least a truce, together.

If the conflict involves the whole group, I have had all-group meetings to bring the issue into the open for discussion. Above, Cynthia references such a situation in Taos. On that particular occasion, a few teens came to me to let me know of ongoing back-biting. When I asked them how they envisioned handling the situation, one of the boys asked permission to lead the group in a short devotion and prayer before beginning a meeting that night. Jason read to the group a Bible passage that he felt reflected the attitudes that were swamping the group. It was a powerful moment for the youth, and after some discussion we stood in a circle and closed with a prayer. That night every single person prayed as they held hands. Primarily, the challenges we experienced on these trips would be better categorized as "drama," usually stemming from personality differences. Your best weapon is to listen with care and love, seeking to resolve the issue. If that does not work, at least help the parties establish a measure of peace, extract an apology, agree to disagree, or find some way to move on.

Try to keep the drama contained between the two individuals. Don't let it escalate to the point that others get involved and take sides. It takes wisdom, patience, and energy to help teens work through these moments. Common sense would dictate that work groups be shifted the next day if the two parties had been working side-by-side.

Escalation is not a pretty thing and results in more hurt feelings, so it needs to be addressed whenever it crops up, even if it requires you to sit on a curb at 2:00 a.m. in front your motel room in Eureka Springs, Arkansas with a crying teen whose hurt feelings prompted her to come and get you. A conversation with the two parties semi-resolved the problem but feelings were so strong that it demanded an adult listening ear for a while. Listen and be supportive even if no solution emerges.

There are times when you will have to make unpopular decisions and the conflict is between you and your own group. When one of our teens wrenched a knee on a hike during our free time, the visit to the ER resulted in an uncertain diagnosis regarding possible damage to her ACL. Parents were called and were not worried about her and said she could stay in NM with us. However, the other adults and I worried that staying with us would delay getting a more precise diagnosis at home and felt a responsibility to get help for her. In addition, being on crutches at the work site was a danger. Most of the youth begged us to let her stay as did she, but we adults ultimately felt it was in her best interest to fly home and get more timely care. That decision was not popular but that is the role we adults are required to play. That night we had a group conversation about the decision, letting the youth express their point of view and us express ours. Even in hindsight, it was the best decision for her and for the group whose focus could return to what we had come to do.

If another group is scheduled to work alongside your group on a project, the potential for conflict is there. Our first college trip to work with Habitat in Taos, NM in 2001 was one such situation. Our small group worked alongside a group of retirees who lived at the work site in their RVs. They had already been there for a week or two and therefore were more familiar than we were with the tasks that needed to be done. The first two workdays were difficult as the retirees seemed to view our young folks as "fresh" labor. Several of them barked orders to our young people, telling (not asking) them to go get this, hand me that, take this to the roof, etc. As our group debriefed in the evenings, it became obvious that though our young people had done what they were told, they greatly resented it.

When both groups assembled on the work site with the job supervisor on the third workday to check-in and learn our assignments for the day, I told the entire gathering that the young people had come to help build a home and were excited to be there and to work hard. Though they felt they had much to learn from the more experienced hands there, the tone of the requests for help was causing resentment, and none of us had heard a "please" or "thank you." As I suspected, the retirees were unaware of how they came across. Immediately there were apologies and expressions of concern. The rest of our time together was pleasant. It was too much to expect the young people to confront their elders, so my role was to be an advocate for them. My comments raised awareness of what had transpired from our point of view and cleared the air for a healthier sense of camaraderie.

A few years later, another college trip to Taos resulted in a group build with retirees once again. This experience was incredibly positive as the older folks invited our younger adults to help them with different tasks and to solve construction problems together. They worked closely as partners with us, even exchanging email addresses at the end of the trip.

BUILDING COMMUNITY WITH EACH OTHER

*From the second we left the parking lot of the church, we began
some intense community building. It was usually pretty early;
so some would listen to some music or squeeze in a little more
sleep. But it didn't take long for some type of game to begin
in the van that usually involved everyone. The games were
even played between the two vans we were separated in. We
had CB radios and in the later years some two-way radios that
allowed each van to communicate with the other van. There
was a practical purpose for the radios but they served an even
greater purpose. Our youth group was split up in vans for
hours; however we remained connected and stayed in constant
laughter. As we played the games we learned who liked what
type of music, who knew all the movies, who the sports fans
were, who the history buffs were, and I learned more about
Pokémon characters than I ever dreamed of. When the games
were on pause, conversations among the youth and adult
sponsors were always happening. I don't recall the specific
conversations but I definitely recall my adult sponsors taking
great interest in what was going on in my life and listening to
whatever else I had to say. I always felt like I was talking with
a friend rather than some authority figure.*

*Once we arrived at our destination, the community building
never stopped. As I think back on the activities we did, I can
hardly think of anything we did that didn't build community.
Everything from the huge puzzles, to the giant pictures we
colored, to the preparation and cleanup of our meals all drew
our youth group closer. We didn't all leave these mission trips
as best friends but 99% of the time we left better friends who
understood each other and appreciated our differences more.*

SETH: four high school and one college trip, 1995-2003; adult sponsor in 2004

*I'm lost. I'm confused. I'm angry. I'm doubtful. All of that is
happening at the same time I am trying to hold myself together
in front of my family, friends, sponsors, and all. Two months prior
to the mission trip to Farrell-Sherard, Mississippi my brother*

passed away. His death was such a catastrophe in my life and something that changed it forever. Battling the waves of emotions that were flowing through me was something that I knew at one point would arise and be something I would need to deal with.

It was that Thursday night during or after the Bible study. I don't know what it was or really how it came about, but all of a sudden I felt a sense of comfort. The people sitting next to me, across from me, and all around had their eyes, ears and hearts open. I began to speak about what had happened and as tears streamed down my face I could barely say another word. As I stumbled through my emotional release, the sense of comfort evolved into openness. All the people around me had known Michael and many of them had gone to the funeral. But for the first time they heard first-hand how losing your brother can change your world.

The evening this occurred affected me forever. It was the first time in my life I felt I was surrounded by people that accepted me for who I was and the things that had happened in my life. I believe this could have occurred at almost any time because my emotions were prepared to explode, but it wasn't until I was with people that had known me my entire life that I was able to release the tension that had been growing inside me. I credit my ability to open up and confide in those around me to some kind of presence. It's hard to explain what it was, except to say…God.

The week began as it usually does. Wake up early, eat breakfast, have devotional, head to the worksite, meet our foreman, begin work, lunch, back to work, and then head home for a shower, dinner, Bible session, and free time. Every day was similar to the one before it. You work as hard as you can and then you spend quality time with the other members of the youth group. As the week progresses, you begin to open up and discuss deeper issues that have been bothering you and your faith. Then all of a sudden…God presents himself to the group and to you. He had been there all along, but it wasn't until a special time that you began to feel his true presence.

I believe this mission trip brought everyone closer together. The things that were said and the way people opened up showed the presence of God. People reached the point of ultimate trust with one another and it was the community and sense of family that allowed us to confide in one another. The sense of community that was created was exactly what we needed. It was exactly what I needed. The week seemingly ended so quickly and I'm pretty sure everyone wanted to stay another week. However, no matter how short our time was together it was clearly worth all the effort and sweat we put into it.

MARK: four high school, one college trip, 2004-2010

TRAVEL TIME

We usually had two fifteen-passenger vans traveling in tandem. In the '90s we had CB radios with which to communicate, and later we used walkie-talkies. These made for easy conversations back and forth and were used for games between vans. One of the traditional games played has no name as far as I know. One van would start with a movie and movie star (Top Gun/ Tom Cruise). The other van would need to respond with the same movie and a different actor or the same actor and a different movie (either Top Gun/Kelly McGillis or Tom Cruise/Mission Impossible I). The idea was to maneuver the choices towards a little known movie or a movie with little known stars that someone in your own van knew about. As adult sponsor Wayne says, "That game sure ate up the asphalt." The other frequent game between vans was to go through the alphabet naming cars, taking turns with each letter. The whole van would get involved in thinking ahead to which letter, thus a car, their van would get next. Much of the time on the road was spent just visiting, but games do help in a lull.

FREE TIME

In my mind, one of the most crucial issues in choosing accommodations is a gathering space where visiting, games, Bible study, and reviewing the day can take place. After a day of work, downtime is essential. As folks await their turn in the showers, they play outside (basketball or Frisbee, depending upon the facilities), go for a short walk (in groups and with an adult if necessary), play cards (Spades is a favorite for us) or games such as "Apples to Apples." If there is table space, we usually take along a jigsaw puzzle and/or a large line-art poster to color (which is signed by everyone and laminated to be hung in the youth lounge at the church). The latter two items are easy "go-to" activities that do not require sustained conversation if one is not so inclined.

After supper and after the evening Bible study, all sorts of card games tend to happen along with informal groups gathering to chat. Group games, impromptu "talent" shows, Spoons, and much laughter are part of the downtime. The inevitable trip to WalMart takes place one evening. In all of the above, the adults are to remain alert to anyone feeling left out.

CONVERSATIONS AT SUPPER

Many of our meals are prepared together and eaten at the Volunteer Center or facilities where we are staying. A routine for us is to have a "check-in" time during the meal with everyone encouraged to participate by sharing the funniest moment of their day or a moment when they felt a sense of accomplishment. The stories are accompanied by lots of laughter and the addition of details by those who witnessed the event that is being described. Because the questions are non-threatening, everyone participates, and it becomes a time of affirmation for all. Deeper sharing of faith-filled experiences usually happens in the evening during the Bible Study/Worship time.

MORNING DEVOTIONS, EVENING BIBLE STUDY/ WORSHIP, DRAWING NAMES FOR PRAYER

More will be said about these activities in Chapter 5, but each in its own way draws the group closer together and contributes to spiritual unbinding as faith issues are explored.

AFFIRMATION CARDS/SHEETS

Everyone loves to be affirmed by others, and one special way to do that is to put it in writing. These affirmations can be taken home and read again and again. At the beginning of the week, make the purpose of the sheets or cards clear, which is to record funny moments with that individual, powerful moments of work shared, or insights gained about the other. The only reminder to everyone is that these are "affirmation" comments, not a time to write down something sarcastic or rude.

On the earlier trips that I organized, the groups were smaller, so having a large sheet of construction paper for each participant sufficed. At the top of each sheet was a person's name (teens, adults, and job supervisor or other local person with whom we worked). These sheets were taped to a blank wall with tape that would not pull off the paint when removed and a bucket of colored markers was placed on the floor beside the sheets so folks could add comments at their leisure during the week. We used thick construction paper and fine point water-based markers so the ink would not bleed through. During the week everyone would add comments so that each person would have a thought from everyone else on their sheet.

As the groups grew in size, there was not enough room on the sheets for everyone to write a comment, so we began to use cards—one for each person in the group for each participant. An explanation as to how these cards were organized is in Chapter 6 which includes a "to do" list for trips.

These affirmation cards or affirmation sheets are wonderful keepsakes to take home and remember the fun times. Reminders will need to be made during the week about the importance of writing a note to each person. This can be done without nagging! Among the supplies for the trip, I would take extra sheets of white construction paper to make large "cards" for the wonderful local people who worked alongside us. Every participant would sign these and on the last afternoon at the worksite we would give the card to those with whom we had worked.

> *I LOVED the affirmation posters in the hall for each person —where others could leave you little notes during the trip. I am pretty sure I still have mine. It was always so exciting to see all the kind and funny things people had to say about me. I remember being (somewhat) a dramatic teen—having a hard day and going back to my room to read those posters.*
>
> KARLY: youth, five trips from 1995 to 2000

> *The affirmation sheets were a great part of the mission trips. I kept mine all throughout high school and college, and would pull them out when I wanted to reminisce. Affirmations are a great idea for high school students who are still trying to figure out who they are; receiving such positive comments from people in the group makes such a difference. It is often others who see our God-given gifts and bring them out in us.*
>
> KARA: four high school and two college trips from 1996-2004; adult sponsor in 2007

One tradition that we always had during mission trips was doing affirmations for each other. The adult sponsors were included and I have to admit that in some ways I looked forward to reading what the adults wrote almost more than what the other youth wrote. I still have many of those affirmations stored in a file cabinet and from time to time I pull them out and read them. Affirmations were meaningful to read because of all the positive words, but they also taught me lessons about myself. Oftentimes, several people would say similar things about me that I never realized about myself. Affirmations were an excellent tool for helping us to realize the many gifts God had blessed us with. Not only did the affirmations cause us to feel good about ourselves, they were a valuable lesson in seeing the gifts in others. It is so easy to see the things in people we don't like or the obvious things we do like. By pausing and thinking about a person for even just a few moments, I learned that we could see good in everyone in very unique and special ways.

SETH: four high school, one college trip from 1995 to 2003; adult sponsor 2004

When I first started to go to NorthPark Church, it was strictly because my grandparents, with whom I was living at the time, told me I had to go. When attending the youth group and Sunday School, I was not happy. My first perception was, "Everyone here is nice…they must be faking it." As time went by, and the more I attended, I realized most of those kids were genuine. For me, that was interesting. As I look back on my friends during my high school years, I realize they weren't my true friends. We were heavily involved in alcohol and other drugs. We never truly cared for each other and I never viewed myself as a "good" person. But these individuals at NorthPark…they seemed to actually care and view me as good even though I knew if they really spent twenty-four hours with me they would quickly change their minds!

When the opportunity arrived to visit Mississippi and work for Habitat for Humanity, I jumped at it. My grandparents were both from Mississippi and I felt it might bring me to connect to their roots. On our last days there, we had these affirmation sheets with our names on them. The purpose was for each individual to write down a memory or a compliment about the others on the trip. I can't recall exactly what I put on peoples' sheets or what was put on mine. However, I do know that the words and thoughts written about me were from the heart. The words used by my peers and adults were humbling. I know that because for the first time in my life I felt sincere, and acted accordingly.

When I arrived back in Dallas, it didn't take long for me to go back to the life I had led. I didn't like it, but that's all I knew to do in my hometown with my "friends." But I kept my affirmation sheets on the wall in my room as a reminder of what I really am...a good person with a heart for others. If no one else saw the true me, I know at that time and at that place in Mississippi the real "me" came bursting through and people saw it and recognized it.

RYAN: two high school and one college trip between 1997 and 2002

TRADITIONS DEVELOP

Drawing names for prayer, the youth leading morning devotions, evening Bible study, faith discussions and particular activities such as Spades, a trip to WalMart, a trip video to be edited and shown to the congregation, thank-you postcards to financial supporters, and returning to places we have been before so we can renew our relationships with the local folks from previous trips are all traditions that can develop over time. This kind of continuity from year to year shapes memories and breeds excitement.

Sometimes it is fun to establish funky traditions such as the mandatory (or at least try it once) snack of peanut butter and a dill pickle slice on a cracker. This began as a silly way to put salt back into our systems after a day of work, but evolved into an anticipated (by most) treat. On later trips, an older youth often would remind me to put the ingredients on a grocery list.

Another tradition I planned was for us to see one goofy or unusual thing each trip. For many years on our way back home we took an extra day for play. Among the most memorable sights: Cadillac Ranch outside

Amarillo, Texas, the ducks parading back to their penthouse at 5:00 p.m. at the Peabody Hotel in Memphis, TN, the former IQ Zoo (where animals did tricks but alas, it has closed) in Hot Springs, Arkansas, and Margaret's Bible Study and Grocery Store outside of Vicksburg, Mississippi. Some of the sights I found on www.roadsideamerica.com, which offers a smorgasbord of the wild and crazy! Our first attempt at this was a stop to see the Peabody ducks in Memphis on our way to Nashville Habitat. When I received my first complaint about how ridiculous the ducks sounded, my mantra for future trips began: "The ducks will be your measuring stick for the whole trip. From here on out each thing we do can be labeled as 'better than the ducks' or 'worse than the ducks.' " Since then any naysayers have been encouraged to use whatever we saw as a measuring stick for everything we did on the trip.

Over the years we did experience meaningful sights as well. Our mid-week afternoon off in the Mississippi Delta usually included a trip to the Clarksdale Blues Museum and/or a trip to Memphis to take in the Civil Rights Museum at the Lorraine Hotel where Dr. Martin Luther King, Jr. was assassinated. The first year we went to the Civil Rights Museum was particularly poignant as our college and high school groups were completing the Farrell, Mississippi community center so that the residents would have a place to vote in the June election.

BUILDING COMMUNITY WITH LOCAL RECIPIENTS

Getting to know the stories of those whom we meet on our trip is an important factor in broadening our worldview. The lives of some of the recipients reflect experiences we have never had in our insular world. One year when we were in the Mississippi Delta you could have heard a pin drop as Ben, a local man who had been helping us learn to drywall, told the group about the way some white men tracked his wife as she drove through the little town of Moon Lake on her way to work. One day someone backed out of their driveway at the exact moment she drove by. Gratefully, the resulting car wreck did not send her and her vehicle into the lake across the street nor was she seriously hurt. Our youth were wide-eyed, not realizing that this sort of thing still happens in today's world.

As adult sponsor Gary comments:

> *The world view of a youth is remarkably narrow and self-centered. Mission trips help to stretch this world view. I was*

often struck by youth descriptions of "major" problems that really just centered around a friend who had snubbed them or a difficult teacher. But to them, this was their whole world. Mission trips help redirect some of this attention to the friends around them and service to the community they were working in. For the average youth who grows up in relatively privileged circumstances, working in the middle of a community of people who are desperately poor helps to broaden the way they see the world.

Each of the job supervisors and home recipients has a story to tell. Get to know them and listen to what they have to say. More stories are shared in Chapter 4 regarding the impact some of these wonderful folks had on us.

The memories recalled in this section reiterate the importance of the role of the adult sponsor and community building. These two factors are instrumental in creating an atmosphere for greater openness to unbinding others and being unbound ourselves.

3

UNBINDING:
Living into Our Call to Serve Others

We should know that God has obligated us to one another to help each other; and at least, when we see anyone in need, although we cannot do him the good we would like, that we treat him humanly."[4]

While the mission trip is a response to the Reformed obligation of offering service to those in need, it also changes those who are offering service. These trips raise awareness of the needs around us and offer the opportunity to unbind others, to free them to live into their call as those who belong to God. This unbinding is to be done with sensitivity and compassion, as Calvin said, "humanly." In freeing others, we see our own need to be freed.

One of the joys of continuing mission trips with young people as they move from high school on through college is to observe their growing awareness of the effect of service upon themselves.

Inherent in who we are as Reformed Christians is the call to live in the here and now, serving those in need to God's glory. We believe that "God is working his purpose out in human history. He calls his people to be the instruments of his purpose. His purposes are not simply the salvation of souls but also the establishment of a holy community and the glorification of his name through all the earth. John Calvin stands out in the history of the church as one who was more vividly aware than almost any other of the mighty working of God in human history and of God's call to his people for service in the world."[5]

In one of his sermons, Calvin confirms this notion of the importance of meeting the needs of a community: Not only did Calvin preach on these issues, he acted on them. While living in Geneva, he set up a group to serve as Deacons who were to be responsible for obtaining and dispensing financial aid to the needy. He also set up a social welfare fund to help political refugees, built a hospital and an educational facility that accepted girls, and helped create a sewer system for the city.[6]

My favorite memory would have to be my freshman year of college when I actually was mature enough to work. I got so much out of that experience and it was not just a vacation with my friends, I actually worked. It felt good helping Carl and the family and then being taken seriously by the rest of my friends. I had a blast on all of the mission trips, there's no doubt about it, but I think that was the first step I took to taking myself seriously and I'm happy that it was at mission trip with you and the rest of my close friends.

JENNIE: four high school and one college trip, 2006-2010

Though the trip to Taos was a memorable one, the times in Farrell-Sherard, MS will always be where the memories are the most plentiful and fondly remembered. It became very uplifting to return there after two years and see how the community had progressed and developed. A home on which I had installed siding two years ago was now occupied by a family, and the church that was just having its foundation laid one year would become the congregating mecca of the community two years later.

I believe that returning to the same place and seeing the impact that we, the NorthPark Presbyterians, had on these specific people, was what made the thought of helping others so much more immediately gratifying, for I saw with my own eyes the cause and effect of my work and contribution. The greatest part of it was that I was enjoying myself along the way, surrounded by familiar faces that cared about me and appreciated my company.

SAM: three high school and one college trip, 2000-2004

No words can express my feelings on the last day that I was there. The feeling that I had made a difference in somebody's life and that if everyone made a little contribution to society's needs, I feel that the world would be a better place for the rich and poor. Seeing the owners of the house that I helped build break down and cry because they were so happy that they finally had a place to call their home is the most rewarding and satisfying feeling a person could ever experience.

RYAN: two high school and one college trip, 1997-2002

I remember very clearly bringing in the young boy in whose house we were installing sheet rock and I showed him the room that would be his and the closet where he would hang his clothes and he was so happy because the house they lived in was barely more than a shack. Rocky remembers seeing literally through the walls of their house, the torn wallpaper and dark with a bare bulb hanging from a wire from the ceiling. It was an eye opener that we lived in the most profitable country in the world, and we were not taking care of our own.

SUSAN AND ROCKY: adult sponsors on two trips, 1988 and 1989

I felt a sense of community at that little church in MS where all the community women cooked us a potluck-style dinner. There is where I saw God's presence when we sang Amazing Grace with the people in that little church. That was a time in my life that I felt amazingly close to God, and will cherish it always. It reiterated that we are all one body of Christ, no matter where we come from.

Also, in Mexico, I felt God's presence in the church courtyard when we played basketball and other games in the rain with the kids of the community. That was an awe-inspiring experience too!

STEPHANIE: four high school trips, 1995-1998

On my very first mission trip to Jonestown, Mississippi, I was assigned to the group which was to paint the interior of the home. My crew members and I had a fantastic time tackling our job, while doing good work and learning more about each other. Keeping in mind that this was a high school trip, we may or may not have let some paint "slip" onto each other (by accident, of course). At the end of the day, my bright green shirt ended up being spotted with the cream-colored paint on the wall. I fondly thought of it as a great souvenir from the work and the play we got to take part in that summer. It ended up being much more than that.

Two years go by. The youth group is back in Mississippi, working on a house just down the road from the one on which we worked the previous time in Jonestown. We had spent a long week doing hard work on the house, and it was time to pack up our things to head back to Dallas. I'm already in the van, ready to go back and finally get a shower. But, someone calls my name, telling me to come with them somewhere. I reluctantly move my tired limbs, hoping that wherever we were going was worth it. I learn that we're going down the street to see if the homeowner from the previous years was at home, to see how she was doing. The tiredness flees from my bones, and I start to run.

Miss Willie Ruth Miles was standing outside, vigilantly watching over a brood of children in the front yard. The kids and sponsors who went on the mission trip two years previously flock up to the driveway and introduce ourselves. She keeps a wary eye on us for a few minutes, but eventually invites us inside. We crowd into her home, marveling at the furniture, the pictures on the wall, and the potted plants—all of the things that made the house we built for her a true home. One of our youth sponsors reminisces about the difficulty he had in putting in a door frame. One of my friends recalls digging a ditch for plumbing and how much fun she and the others had. I look at the familiar color of the walls and begin to laugh. Wearing the exact same green shirt that I had those years ago, I walk up to Miss Miles. "Look," I exclaim, and point to a blob of old, dried paint on my shirt, and then point to the wall. The colors matched exactly. She smiled, shook her head in disbelief, and cleared her throat to address the group.

Miss Willie Ruth Miles told us that afternoon about how she was a single mother of eight children and worked multiple jobs to support them. She said how she thanked God every day for us because we were willing to help her when we didn't even know her. We were willing to work for her just through having faith that she needed this home. She thanked us for building this house that she could make into a home. Willie Ruth Miles began to cry, repeating that she was so, so thankful. We all embraced the little woman, reminding her that we were thankful for her, too. After some of my friends dispersed, I approached her to give her a hug of my own. She pointed again to the splotch of paint, shook her head, and said, "I thank God every day."

I learned how to thank God because of Willie Ruth Miles and mission trips. In thin places and everywhere else, I thank Him for the opportunity to serve beautiful people such as these alongside my brothers and sisters in Christ. Nothing is better than that. I thank God every day.

KATIE: three high school trips, 2008-2010

Since my high school days of mission work, I have always taken the opportunity to be a part of that. In college I took different opportunities around Oklahoma to do mission work. As a young married adult without children, we continued to do local daily mission opportunities. But when we started having kids, my mission trip days stood in the front of my mind. It is and has been something I want my kids to desire and be a part of. When Chloe, my now nine year-old, was two and a half, she took dance at a little studio in Downtown Frisco. It was in a strip across the street from an old gas station. Every day a dozen or so Hispanic men (day laborers) would be standing there waiting for work. One day, Chloe said, "We should take them a lollipop and tell them Jesus loves them!" As a new protective mother, with two babies in a stroller next to my two and half year-old, I thought this might not be a good idea! But quickly I realized this could be her first opportunity to see "mission/ or ministry work."

So we did. And for about six months, [until we moved] every Friday we had these men waiting for us. We always arrived with a lollipop, baked cookies, sandwiches, something, and then cards attached telling them the truth of Jesus. I began to look forward to our Fridays with them.

My husband had never done mission work until our church. I honestly was shocked. But more than that, I was sad for him. I couldn't wait for him to have a chance to serve others in this way. He loved it. We have been able to have family mission days and it is just as it was, "We are blessed even more than those we are there to bless." Recently I encouraged him to take his first mission trip away from home. He went to Honduras for a week, and there are not words to explain [his experience]. Our kids are at a [private] school that is very mission focused. In fact they start raising money for their grade levels as early as kindergarten to support the trips they will go on in junior high and high school, local and international. I have promised Chloe just this past year that she can go to Africa in a few years with our vice principal. I hope we can go as a family.

I share what has happened since, because I truly believe the seeds for this were sown back in my high school days of mission trips. It has stayed in my heart as a way to do His work for His people. It has always reminded me that we are not all that different from one another. It gave me a perspective that we just cannot get sitting in our four firm and insulated walls that we live in day to day.

JULIE: two trips, 1990, 1992

Those experiences will forever be etched in my memory and I now often seek to give back and participate in service projects just to see the smile of a grateful person or leave with the self-satisfaction of knowing I can help make someone's situation better when I leave than it was before my arrival. I am currently a second-year medical student and have devoted my life to being a humanitarian and helping those that cannot help themselves. The Habit for Humanity experience was a significant propelling event in my life to initiate my drive for helping others. Today, I still participate in service projects as I accept the call to serve others. I have recently volunteered at a free clinic that offers medical services free of charge to local community members in the DC, Maryland, and Virginia (DMV) area. Freedman's clinic was established to serve the economically disadvantaged and it was an easy choice for me to make to want to become involved. I often see grateful smiles on patients that leave the clinic, smiles that are reminiscent of those families that received homes from Habitat for Humanity. These smiles continue to serve as a reminder that the call to serve is very rewarding. My mission trip experiences truly changed my life and improved so many others.

BRIAN: three trips, 2001-2003

Sometimes we experience a serendipitous moment that draws us together with those we do not even know. Donna, an adult sponsor on four trips from 1997 to 2001, recalls:

My favorite memory was when the kids began to sing in a restaurant in Arkansas as we were traveling back home on a Sunday and the place was busy with patrons who had arrived after worship. Our group was singing at the table and a waitress overheard them and encouraged them to sing for her. They decided to sing "Sanctuary" and didn't realize the entire restaurant would all be listening. Members of a black church were standing in line waiting to pay and began to sing with them, then raised their hands above their heads, giving our youth a standing O. It still gives me chills to think of how quiet the restaurant became and how beautiful the kids sounded, in harmony with another "congregation."

In the mid-1990s as we planned a trip to Farrell-Sherard, Mississippi, I received a call from a Presbyterian pastor from a town in central Mississippi whose group was going to be working with Habitat in another area of the Mississippi Delta. He invited our group to have supper with his group at a parishioner's lake home on nearby Moon Lake where his group was staying. It was an interesting evening. Our youth were eager to meet a new group of kids and even took a cassette player with "energizers" on it so they could teach the Mississippi group their favorite energizer, "Star-Trekking." Not only did the other group watch us be silly and decline to participate with us, they also segregated themselves most of the evening, complaining about wanting to spend less time working with Habitat and more time waterskiing on the lake. The adults from that group were very friendly but none of their youth sat with our youth at dinner or engaged in much conversation with us. On the way home, one of our guys commented that the African Americans in the communities of Sherard and Ferrell were more open and friendly to us than our fellow Presbyterians. Several youth expressed surprise regarding how the other group's mission trip focus was so different from ours. A profound discussion followed on what we are to be about as servants of Christ.

This same young man who initiated that conversation is now a pastor serving a Presbyterian church. Rev. Joshua Robinson recalls:

> I do remember the community of the folks we were there to serve, and I remember there being a richer sense of authenticity in their relationships and humble understanding of what it means to be served [than the other church group]. During seminary, I took a group of very wealthy young people on a mission trip to Mexico. We flew to San Diego, rented vans, and drove from there to Ensenada. As we approached the border, the privileged young people started talking, ridiculing Mexicans for being lazy and impoverished plagues on our society, and I flat out slammed the brakes on the van and pulled it to the side of the highway and had an out of body, "come to Jesus" experience with them. What I learned from that trip, which was very well reflected in the other group we met in Mississippi, is what it means when Jesus says that he didn't come to be served but to serve. We as westernized Americans have created and developed a specific culture of being served and struggle mightily with what it means to serve others. And also, because we have embraced a culture of individualism, we have nearly completely forgotten that the peace of Christ that is shared with us in his love exists only when we realize that we are bound up in each other. My peace

exists only when your peace exists. This is why mission trips are so vital to one's faith journey. Not because we learn how to pity someone else, but because we learn that we are sisters and brothers in Christ, redeemed people of God's choosing.

4. William J. Bouwsma, *John Calvin: A Sixteenth-Century Portrait* (Oxford University Press, 1988), 201.

5. John H. Leith, *Introduction to the Reformed Tradition* (John Knox Press, 1981), 75.

6. William Stacy Johnson, *John Calvin: Reformer for the 21st Century* (Westminster John Knox Press, 2009), 117-18.

4

UNBOUND PERSONALLY
Through Experience and People

Our own healing and spiritual nurturing happens through the relationships on the mission trips, whether those relationships are with the beneficiaries of our work, other youth, or adult sponsors. Realizing that "unbinding" is not a one-way process from "us" to "them" is huge because we middle-class folks tend to have the mindset that we are going on this trip "to help those unfortunate people," a viewpoint that is a travesty to the gospel message. Indeed, unbinding is a mutual process.

The unbinding may take place over a period of time as our awareness expands regarding how God has been at work in us through others, or the unbinding may offer us a momentary glimpse of the Kingdom of God, which gives us a new perspective on our lives. The trips can be a time of self-awakening or self-reflection as we serve and see God at work. Below, the stories of three adults and two youth demonstrate the life-changing frame-of-reference they experienced on mission trips.

> *The trips unbound me from the judgments about myself and from thinking I was trapped and unforgivable. I was able to get the answers I needed to make big changes in my life. I felt like God showed me His way, not my way. It was difficult, but led me to a much better place where I could make God the priority in my life. I also gained lasting friendships and the desire to serve others as an adult. After [my first] trip, when we arrived at the church, my tears just poured because I knew I had to go back to my life and the mess I had created.*

I felt completely trapped in my life. The next day, I felt God's presence again and knew that I could leave that life and get back on His path, and I did. It was very clear that He had other plans for me.

After the trip, I had to make a choice: a fuller life with God leading the way or the life I had with God as a part of it. I chose to follow God, and with that choice coming right on the heels of the mission trip, I felt very connected to the youth group. I told them about the changes I decided to make, and they were very supportive and accepting. It was difficult for me because I was their leader, and I wanted them to make good choices and follow God's plan from the beginning. I had gotten off the path, and I had to divorce a man to turn back to God. I think many people take marriage less seriously than they should, and I didn't want to be a statistic. I realized though that God didn't want to lose me or throw away His plan for me. I made a mistake, but I wasn't unforgivable, and He gave me a chance to start fresh. Going through this humbling transition in my life brought me closer to the youth and church as a whole. I never felt judged, just loved. I needed that kind of support to accept God's grace. The church members' and youth's hugs made me feel like I was still a part of the community. They helped me heal.

CHERYL: two trips as adult sponsor, 1995, 1996

When I advanced to the high school group, we alternated between trips to Mississippi and New Mexico, where we worked with Habitat for Humanity. Over those years, we built relationships and partnerships with site coordinators, families, and communities that benefited from the homes we helped build. But, by far, my favorite part of these trips was fellowshipping with the people in the community. It was in these moments that I always felt more like the recipient of Good News rather than the provider of it. It was in these exchanges that I believed what scripture tells us: each person is given the manifestation of the Spirit for the benefit of the common good.

It has been nearly fifteen years since that first mission trip experience…and I am now a candidate for ordination in the Presbyterian Church (U.S.A.). God has been unbinding me all these years. My hobby of attending mission trips has turned into a calling. With my Masters in Divinity and my Masters in Social Work, I hope to pursue community outreach ministry on behalf of a church.

KRISTI: three high school and three college trips, 2003-2010

Sophomore year in high school was a really dark and hard time for me. For some reason I just started struggling and didn't really care much about anything: school, family, friends and even church. I wasn't really sure to whom I could turn to try and help get me back on track. At the end of the year everyone started talking about mission trips and I wasn't excited and I wasn't planning on going. One, money was a problem in my family and I didn't think it was even going to be possible to go on the trip and I didn't really see the point anymore. I got a phone call that week from Jann telling me that there was a family that was willing to help pay for the missing amount that my parents couldn't afford. At first I wasn't excited, I didn't want to go, I didn't want to put a smile on my face for a whole week with everyone around me.

The week of mission trip came and we got in the vans to start heading off to Mississippi. When we got there I couldn't believe how different the world was there. There were houses just torn down, missing doors, windows, parts of roofs, and it made me feel sad and so powerless. One of my really good friends that I was the closest with could just see the look on my face looking out the window and said, "We just don't know how lucky we are." I remember thinking, "Yeah, sure."

As the week went by I had a chance to talk more with my good friend and I told her I was really struggling and she held my hand and told me that sometimes all it takes is being able to admit that you need help. That week was over and it was really hard to come home. My family was still having troubles and I tried to keep a smile on but when I was lying in bed at night I would just close my eyes and remember that week and it would help me. I would just lie in bed staring at my ceiling talking to God. It really wasn't always praying, it was more like telling him about my day and what I needed help with that night. I felt I was talking to a friend. I think what mission trips really did for me was help me to realize that God is this almighty power but we don't have to be afraid of him. I needed a friend to help me and even if I didn't have complete faith, I knew he would be there listening.

On these trips I grew closer to a lot of the youth and that felt good. It felt like I finally had a group, like I was part of something. I felt like part of the family! Having these friends with me even if we were all only together a week was the most amazing family anyone could ask for. I shared things with them and everyone shared their stories. We were all so open with each other and no one was left out or forgotten. For that one week we all needed each other in some way and we were all there for each other no matter whether we were thrown out of the water-rafting boat [in Taos] or just needed help lifting something. We all worked as a team.

I'm so blessed to have been on four mission trips and I remember every single second of working that hard and knowing that it helps me a lot today. I work full time and go to school with an eighteen-hour load, but looking back at those mission trips I know that I am strong and that [no matter what is] thrown at me at any time, I have my friends, my family, and a loving Father who will always be waiting for me to talk to the ceiling, which of course I still do! —

JAMIE: four trips, 2007-2010

Within the church, all of us try to find our niche, to find a place where we can use our gifts. I am someone who was raised and brought up in the church. My whole life I felt the purpose of me going to church was to just be a "good" Christian. My only problem was that I did not know how to accomplish this. I could never just sit down and read the Bible, and I never have been one to keep up with giving pledges to the church. In my house there is no exception…everyone goes to church, so basically going to church every Sunday just became a weekly habit.

Unfortunately as I grew older and made it into the senior high room, I still didn't know, or even care about giving off "a good Christian vibe." I hate to say it, but by the time I was in Jr. High, I honestly felt like I was just taking up space in the pews on Sunday mornings. Not long after, though, I went on my first mission trip and realized what Christianity could be about.

On that trip I learned that being a strong Christian isn't just about being able to recite Bible verses or give money to the community. It is about finding your own way to serve Christ. And for me, that service became meaningful through physical labor to help others have a home. There are few words to express what I felt when I saw the look on the faces of the Habitat families we served. I have to say that after we finished a house my freshman year, my perspective about the church and the church's work completely changed. It was an unbelievable experience. Working on my first mission trip showed me a way to share my faith with others.

BRADEN: three trips, 2008-2010

I learned that good hard labor allows us to learn a lot about ourselves. You can achieve a lot more by working together… sometimes a hard task was finally accomplished by working as a team. One of my favorite memories from high school: Jessica and I attempting to use our awesome geometry skills to create the perfectly sized triangle of siding to finish a wall of our Habitat house in Kansas City. She and I worked REALLY hard together, trying to determine the lengths of all the sides. We then created a template, cut out the siding, and gave it a go. I think it only took us two tries (and like two hours), but we had a great time solving our dilemma.

KARA: four high school and two college trips, 1996-2004; adult 2007

UNBOUND BY RECIPIENTS AND JOB SUPERVISORS IN THE COMMUNITIES

I continue to marvel over what I/we have learned from the residents of the communities we have gone to serve. They have offered examples of how I understand God to be working in our broken world and we come away from those experiences changed for the better. Each job supervisor/volunteer coordinator at the work site, each recipient of a home, and each member of the community where we serve has a story. Forming relationships with them as we work, worship, and play will broaden our worldview and will personalize daily struggles that we have heard about only from a distance in the news.

Two people in the Mississippi Delta community have touched our lives immeasurably, partly due to our many years of experience with them: Dorothy Jenkins, on the Farrell-Sherard Habitat Board and Carl Fuller, the Habitat job supervisor in the Delta. Others in Habitat leadership positions showed us devotion to their task and support for us. They had an impact as well, though our interaction with them was less: Juanita Burnett of Jonestown, Paul Hesch, Kyle Berry, Cynthia Arvidson, and Rick Martin of Taos Habitat.

Dorothy would greet us our first night with her laughter and warmth, stating "Welcome to the family you never knew you had." That warmth reflected the attitude of the whole Farrell-Sherard community. Carl, the job supervisor there and later at Jonestown, always shared a bit of his story and his steadfast faith in God's presence and guidance. In the midst of that, he taught us the virtue of doing our best as we worked on homes for others. He insisted that we were not to step back from our work and say, "That's good enough." Avoiding that one phrase helped us to take more pride in our work. The impact of these two servants of God is described further by Gary, adult sponsor on 12 trips:

> For all of us taking mission trips to Mississippi in the 1990s and early 2000s, Dorothy Jenkins embodied the type of experience we would have. She was the face of the Farrell-Sherard Habitat organization; the first person we saw; the person who made us feel welcome and important; and the person who gave real meaning to why we were there. One of the things that at first startled, and then delighted, our Presbyterian city kids was her very open "God talk," the casual and habitual

mentioning of God, the grace of God in her life; her hope for the grace of God in your life; the many blessings that God had bestowed on her life, etc. Our group was not used to hearing this! With other people in our lives, it might feel insincere, like a television evangelist trying to raise money, but with Dorothy, it was genuine.

Dorothy made all of us feel loved. She was truly thankful for our help, and said so warmly and openly. When we had prayers of dedication, she was emotional, sometimes moved to tears. Everyone felt her warmth, and through her leadership, the whole Farrell-Sherard Habitat organization showered their love on all of us. I can honestly say that none of us ever felt any racial divide working in Mississippi. We were always treated as "one of them." One of the ways they showed their love for us was by the community dinner that the group would treat us to on Thursday nights. Good old Southern cooking at its best! Fried chicken, lots of greens and—Teola's chocolate cake that quickly gained a reputation in our group!

For many years, our work supervisors came and went in Mississippi, but when Carl Fuller arrived, a sense of permanency and continuity prevailed. Carl is a small example of what is increasingly happening in the South. He is a Southern African American who moved north, had a long and successful career, and then moved back to his native South in retirement years. In Carl's case, he had worked for the Port Authority of New York, and left his job in the aftermath of 9-11. Though he had never been to Mississippi, he read about the need for a Habitat for Humanity job supervisor in the MS Delta and responded. He felt he could "make a difference" in a state to which he had never been but that very much needed his help.

Carl was not a builder or construction professional, but he had worked with young people and brought a natural tendency to network, to connect people, to find resources, and to get things done. He was warm and kind, and genuinely liked teenagers. He understood that although work needed to be done, the larger mission on some trips was the further development of the wonderful teens who were in his charge for a week. Carl taught the teens by example, stressing safety, the need to take breaks, and the need to take their work seriously. He showed that the work they were doing was much more than just, for example, painting an empty room—the teens were actually providing a new bedroom, possibly the first real bedroom, for a little girl.

Carl was always pulled in a million directions, and sometimes the teens would grow frustrated at the slow pace of their work as they waited for needed supplies like paint brushes or ladders. But this was part of their learning experience, the experience of seeing how things happen in the real world where supplies are not readily available and where trucks sometimes break down or run out of gas.

GARY

And Amy shares:

Growing up in a predominantly Caucasian, middle-class city, I was shown by my parents and church that as fellow humans, we should lend our abilities to help others who, for whatever reasons, had fallen on hard times. Through things such as food drives, toy drives, and fundraisers, I had a general awareness that I was blessed and there were people for whom life was a struggle, but I had never truly understood or experienced it until our mission trip to Coahoma. There were several moments from the week spent in Coahoma that changed my perspective and still influence the choices I make today.

The moment that had the most impact on me was when the Habitat for Humanity house we had been working on was almost ready and the family that was going to live there came by to walk through it. I remember how excited the little girl was to have her own room, how excited the mom was to have a working kitchen and to be able to do laundry indoors, how happy they were to have sturdy walls and floors. All things that until then, I had either taken for granted or assumed that most people had...at least all the people I knew. I suddenly gained a new appreciation for the things in life that we sometimes forget are not guaranteed, but luxuries. That is something that really stuck with me. Even now, twenty years later, I try not to lose sight of this lesson and try not to get caught up in chasing the "things" that the American society uses to define success. I am grateful every day to have a safe place to live, heating and air conditioning, running water, and grocery stores full of choices...all things these families didn't necessarily have.

I also remember riding in the van with our church group and a group of the Coahoma kids to go to the small general store for a soda. The children were looking at us and touching our faces saying things like "your hair is strange" and "your noses look different than ours." Funny how in my world, they would be the different ones, but in their world, we were the different ones. That was my first true lesson in diversity and recognizing and respecting the uniqueness of cultures other than my own.

AMY: two trips, 1989 and 1991

All of the mission trips I went on have impacted me, but I think the one that impacted me the most was when we went to Farrell-Sherard, Mississippi. I believe we were all meeting in a local church for lunch and Jennie and I had decided to go out and play with some of the local girls to pass the time. They were fascinated by how long our hair was and just kept playing (tangling it in knots) with it, they were so sweet and you could tell that their current living situation had no effect on their dreams. A couple of girls kept telling us about how they wanted to be doctors and lawyers. It was truly inspiring to see them with these aspirations. It really gave the mission trip more meaning. Meeting the families and the people being helped by Habitat for Humanity is touching but just spending 30 minutes with these girls made the work that we were doing mean so much more.

CHANELLE: three trips, 2007-2009

Usually we would have some type of closing worship or dedication service with those whom we were serving. I was constantly amazed by the positive and grateful attitudes of those we were serving. I will never forget the hospitality and amazing cooking the people in Mississippi treated us to. It was hard for me to understand why people who were so poor would give so much to us. They demonstrated first-hand how money and possessions aren't what make you happy. They demonstrated how you didn't need a big fancy church building or hundreds of members to have a strong congregation. Lastly, they demonstrated the impact one strong and faithful person can have on a community and the visitors of their community. I would guess that not one person who met Dorothy would ever forget her smile, her graciousness, and most of all her voice as she sang "Amazing Grace."

SETH: FIVE youth and college trips, 1995-2003; adult in 2004

Regarding Nashville, the trip where we learned to install siding, we remember Mr. Campbell, the job supervisor who was an educator and shop teacher at a public high school. This man bravely and oh so patiently, taught us what the heck we were doing.

ROCKY and SUSAN: adult sponsors, two trips, 1988, 1989

I remember Mr. Campbell from the Nashville trip. He was the construction manager and his people skills were as good as they come. He could get people to do things without telling them to do it. As a school board member I wish I had his abilities.

MIKE M: two trips, 1988 and 1990

[Going to Mexico] showed me how fortunate I was in growing up in a middle-class suburb in Dallas. I stayed with a family that appeared to be a typical middle-class family in Mexico, yet it showed me what a relatively pampered life I lead. Their refrigerator was nearly empty except for basics and what would be eaten in the next day or two. There also was no wasting of food. I vividly remember a severely cracked egg that had oozed some contents but was still sitting in the egg crate to be used later. At home, that egg would have been thrown away and the fridge and pantry always had a plethora of choices of food

and drinks. They had one black and white TV in the house that was smaller than the color TV I had in my bedroom back home. The house either didn't have a/c or it wasn't enough to cool the house properly. The family welcomed us in with open arms and provided everything we needed, but it was not what I was used to.

This particular trip showed me that "church" is not a building or a place, it is a group of people. The people we helped had a small one-room building to worship in and a couple of classrooms that I believe groups before us built. The classrooms were mostly bare with very worn chairs and desks. If memory serves, there was not glass in most of the windows. Despite not having the nice sanctuary, multiple rooms, and offices we had at home, they had the same sense of community that we had (maybe even better) and just as effectively served the Lord. Their church seemed to be the center of their life, not where you go only on Sunday morning.

In summary, the trips created many great memories…playing hide and seek in the church in Memphis, the sites in Mexico, the smiles on the congregation's faces in Mexico, to name a few. But the one thing that sticks with me the most is the image of that cracked egg in the refrigerator in Merida, Mexico and what an incredibly lucky person I am.*

BRENT: two trips, 1987, 1988

*Note: The trip to Merida took place the year before I began organizing trips.

One of the best parts of these trips was connecting with the families we were helping. We got to work side by side with these families, learning about their lives and stories. More often than not, I was blown away by the fact that the families were concerned about giving back to others. The community was so supportive of one another.

Another favorite memory would have to be dancing in the rain with the kids in Piedras Negras, Mexico. The soothing rain was such a blessing to us and the town. After many scorching hot days, it was so refreshing to play out in the rain—to let *loose and be a kid. They reminded us not to take ourselves too seriously and to live in the moment.*

KARA: four trips as a youth, two as a college student, 1996-2004; adult 2007

There was an old gentleman who lived on the road to Clarksdale, MS for whom we were building a home. When his current landlords found out he was going to get a Habitat House, they cut off his water. This necessitated him driving into Clarksdale every day to buy large containers of water for cooking, drinking, and if any was left over, bathing. It was about the same time that they discovered either he or his wife had cancer. I still remember him being happy and not the least bit downtrodden. He saw God at work to give him a home rather than appearing bitter about his treatment.

The most meaningful occurrence for me was in Taos. We were having a picnic one evening [with the recipients of Habitat homes]. One of our helpers was an Indian and his extended family was there with him. His niece and nephew collided while playing, and she complained of severe back pain. We rushed her to the hospital and spent about four hours with the family while they ran various tests.

It was such a meaningful evening for me because of my intense interest in American Indians. During that vigil I was able to talk with the young girl's mother, aunt, grandmother and grandfather. The aunt confided in me the intense pressure that exists in trying to live by the rules of the Pueblo society and yet exist in the modern Anglo world. It meant so much to me to see how the family gathered around in time of trouble just as any of our families would do. Thank goodness the little girl turned out to be okay. Although we didn't share conversations about our religious beliefs, I know they would have been extremely different. I felt very close to God that evening and continue to thank him for the opportunity to spend such quality time with one of my "sisters."

WAYNE: adult, ten trips from 1995 to 2005

A GLIMPSE OF THE KINGDOM OF GOD IN COAHOMA, MISSISSIPPI

The second youth mission trip I organized was in 1989 through Habitat for Humanity in Coahoma, Mississippi, just east of the Mississippi River and north of Clarksdale. One hundred percent of this small community of 350 lived below the poverty level due to lack of any industry in the area. Before we left Dallas, I had been told that the local teenage males wanted to play basketball one evening with our boys as they had a court in the community. Our guys were bragging in the van on the way there, assuming that their advantaged lives gave them a leg up on this skill: "We'll beat the sox off these small town boys." In fairness to our Presbyterian youth, most had never been exposed to this level of poverty and were reflecting our own culture based on competition and the importance of winning. I would hope that we adults attempted to tone down the arrogance but I cannot recall.

What I do remember, though, upon our arrival is clear as a bell. After parking the rental van, our boys were still in a swaggering mode until we walked around the corner of a building and saw the local boys coming towards us. They were tall, lean, muscular and smiling. One of our boys said, "Oh, shit" as he caught sight of the opposition. It was a quiet walk to the basketball court. Once there, the Coahoma boys, knowing, I am sure, that they had the advantage, chose to split themselves into two teams, skins vs. shirts, and to invite our boys to split and join them on the two teams. Thus the local guys played WITH our boys instead of AGAINST them on two evenly matched teams. What a lesson in humility and grace! What the Dallas boys failed to take into consideration is that this run-down basketball court was the center of activity for the youth of the community. They knew how to play. It would have been so easy to have played against us and skunked us, but they intentionally did not to do that. When I picture the Kingdom of God, I envision this basketball game of hospitality, graciousness, inclusion, and laughter.

LESSONS FROM CARMEN IN RANCHO DE TAOS, NEW MEXICO

One of the privileges the NPPC Sr. Highs have had on their mission trips to Taos has been the invitation to participate with the community of Rancho de Taos in their annual ritual of re-mudding the outside of the well-known St. Francis of Assisi Church in early June. We were able to do this five times. It was a pretty incredible experience to be a part of this tradition and work alongside people who have done this for decades. The week we are there, we split into groups, a few of us going every day.

Every year we have been there, we see Carmen, one of the matriarchs of that community who began her work on the church as a child alongside her grandmother. On one trip I asked Carmen to tell me and the group of teens who were there with me the real story of something I had heard about on an earlier trip. I asked her to tell us about the time the church was covered with cement in order NOT to have to continue re-mudding every year.

It seems that in the 1960s discussions began about ways to keep the church from experiencing its constant deterioration that required constant upkeep. The priest of St. Francis at the time began exploring with some businessmen ways to coat the exterior walls with acrylic material that would preserve the walls. Other local folks along with Carmen tried to fight his plan. She and other locals knew that adobe must have air to breathe.

At this point in her re-telling, Carmen leaned over towards us and whispered a blunt statement expressing her feelings: "Fr. ____ didn't know shit from Shinola." The priest's plan prevailed and the process began of applying a cement-type stucco that contained acrylic. In 1967 the new stucco application was completed, but almost immediately it began to crack. By 1970 it was an unsightly mess. Fiberglass fabric tape had been put over the cracks and then painted, but then it too began to split. The cracks allowed water to get under the stucco but not dry out. And so, the water began its unseen work of disintegrating the adobe walls underneath.

A new priest arrived, Fr. O'Brien, who listened to the people. With much cost, time, and effort, the stucco was chipped away only to discover that the damage had reached the adobe bricks deep inside and beyond. The community itself began rebuilding St. Francis in 1979, making 60,000 adobe bricks and beginning the process of mudding over the bricks again as their ancestors had done. The rebuilding was completed in 1980 and the practice of annual re-mudding resumed.

The act of putting cement over adobe bricks to preserve the church resulted in unseen deterioration because adobe, in a sense, is a living thing that needs to breathe. I have been struck, ever since hearing the story, about how we in the church sometimes live in the middle of that story. The image of what happened to St. Francis of Assisi church is the image of what happens when we try to preserve the church, try to keep it just the way it is, try to make it a static institution.

Carmen's story taught me that attempting to preserve the church exactly the way it is stifles the Holy Spirit and its work, and the spirit within its members crumbles as well. It might take us years to realize the damage that has been done. We are called to be a church that is constantly being re-formed, that is a living architecture dependent upon its members, and that allows room for the Holy Spirit to breathe.

Early on in the rebuilding process in the late 1970s, Father O'Brien was asked about the continual efforts at re-mudding that would be required. He replied, "It is a living church, and the first priority must be prayer. The worst thing that could happen to it would be to become a museum." [7] This story causes me to reflect on the church, our programs and even our trips. Do we demonstrate that we are living into our baptismal call by exhibiting openness and new life in Christ or are we trying to hunker down and preserve what we have as we remain wrapped in our grave cloths?

UNBOUND BY OTHER YOUTH AND SPONSORS

> *The trip to Nashville was fun, rewarding, and allowed me to feel some community with the family we helped and with the youth group. I liked the sense of confidence and accomplishment it gave me to pull up to the house with no siding on it and drive away with it almost completed. At the time, the biggest impact was the relationships I built with the youth leaders and the other kids in the youth group. As you would expect spending 5 or 6 or 7 days with the same group, I created some very strong bonds on the trip. I know those strong bonds boosted my participation in future youth group activities.*
>
> BRENT: two trips, 1987, 1988

> *I remember Mississippi my freshman year which was the same year my parents got a divorce. Thursday night after the potluck, we prayed with the people in the community, then began our Bible study. The topic that night triggered much emotion in*

me as I shared my family's struggle. We talked about faith and problems, and I really felt God's presence. At one point I got overwhelmed and had to leave the room, but when a friend encouraged me to return to the group, one of the boys who was better known for his sarcasm than his sensitivity called me over to the couch and hugged me and talked to me. He really helped me a lot that first year with adjusting as he had experienced a divorce in his family as well.

KATIE: three trips, 2006-2009

[During] the school year the Jr. Highs and Sr. Highs were in different classes. Going on mission trips all together really gave me time with people a few grades ahead of me. I feel like I really had people to look up to. And that if they could make it through all the drama of growing up, I could too. It is hard to stay on the "straight and narrow path," so seeing "older" kids who did made it easier for me later on.*

KARLY: five trips, 1995-2000

* Note: Our first two trips at NorthPark included both Jr. and Sr. Highs due to the small size of the group.

During one trip after the Mississippi community shared their faith at dinner, we had our evening Bible study. We told stories of heroes from our lives and I shared the story of my mother before she died. When I was finished, Megan, a new member to our youth group at that time, told me that I must be a very strong person to be able to share that story so openly, even if it was with a group of close friends. Hearing that kindness from an almost total stranger was incredibly encouraging and gave me a confidence in myself.

KATY: four high school and one college trip, 2006-2010

While many kids say that the highlights of their summers are expensive vacations to tropical beaches, weeks spent at extravagant camps in the mountains, or just lying around by the pool, I can speak for myself and many others at NorthPark when I say that the highlight of my summer is our mission trip.

We are privileged enough to work with spectacular people for a spectacular organization, getting down and dirty in building homes for people in need. I've learned countless skills by going on these trips. In my four years, I've tried my hand at painting, mudding, dry walling, and concrete pouring, along with various other odd jobs around houses that we got to help make into homes.

Along with learning interesting things about construction, the weeks spent in Jonestown and Taos were fantastic opportunities for the youth group to bond. I made relationships in those places with those people that I will cherish for the rest of my life. I will never forget the amazing fellowship we shared around meals, card tables, and Bible studies, where we could openly discuss the pain and joy in our lives and in our walks with Christ. In the midst of that community, I had the opportunity to see and experience what it means to not only love, but be loved. My brothers and sisters in Christ worked alongside and with me to build up the strength of my heart and my faith simultaneously with the walls of a home for a family. I am certainly grateful, and the families are, too.

KATIE: three trips, 2008-2010

God is at work through many venues to move us toward wholeness. Mission trips are one way to provide opportunities that unbind us from our self-imposed limitations and short-sighted vision for ourselves and for others, and unbind us from our restrictive views of the ways God functions in this world. Like Lazarus, we are offered new life through these trips as they transform us into more faithful servants.

7. Van Dorn Hooker, *Centuries of Hands: An Architectural History of St. Francis of Assisi Church* (Santa Fe Press, 1996), 75.

5

Planning for Spiritual and Group
NURTURE AND REFLECTION

I 've been a late-bloomer in all things. Adolescence was slow. I didn't attend seminary until I was in my forties and my call to Christian Education came later in mid life. It took me a while to figure out that youth really want real spiritual depth as well. It was not that I avoided "God-talk" with the youth in the early years, but I emphasized the fun angle of Sunday evening fellowship and mission trips. The youth knew even then, though, that our common belief in Jesus Christ was our foundation and serving each other was our call. Instinct and a love of young people prompted me to listen and be open to their questions and doubts, which were so important to address, but there was little intentional planning for deep faith conversations. I was naïve enough to think that the young people would resist deeper Bible study and heavier discussions.

Over the years, God used the youth with whom I worked and the more recent youth ministry research from the late '90s on to unbind me from these formerly held notions and assumptions about the spiritual needs of youth. As I came to realize their deep yearning for faith conversations, I began to address that void tentatively at first, then with gusto. Early on in this transformative journey, one of the youth asked to help plan and lead a Sunday evening youth-led worship service. The excitement generated from this project catapulted me (unbound me) to alter my previous perspectives on what they wanted. I am forever grateful to you, Cecelia!

Morning devotions had always been a part of the early mission trips, but then I began to add dimensions to our trips that resulted in heartfelt conversations and deepening reflections. We added youth-led devotions rather than adult-led, evening worship time/Bible study, and drawing names for prayer during the trip.

The young people began leading morning devotions that reflected a depth of faith, which inspired us all. If some were interested but intimidated by the thought of leading, they took on a partner and would prepare a devotion in pairs. A simple worship time/Bible study in the evenings often led to rich discussions of beliefs and personal sharing of struggles and awakenings. The latter led to opportunities for support of one another and expressions of concern. The trip offered times to celebrate more openly than ever before our affirmation of God's presence and call.

Many readers will have moved far beyond these efforts to a deeper faith experience that touches the lives of their participants. Through their own creativity and wisdom, they have established even more profound activities that enhance the spiritual growth of those with whom they travel. But if you have not explored such matters, I urge you to do so. What I present is a place to begin, not end. Much more can be done with your group as God opens up your imagination to God's Spirit. Even at retirement, I had a mental check list of other things I could have done, not the least of which was to equip the young people to develop their own thematic worship/Bible studies. This proved to be a challenge in the spring due to their school activities, but I believe a way could have been found!

MORNING DEVOTIONS

This activity is student led. At the parent/youth orientation meeting a couple of weeks before the trip, youth are given a chance to volunteer for a particular morning. Most often they work in pairs. The only guideline for those responsible is an invitation to choose a Bible passage and/or song that speaks to them and tell the group why they chose it, allowing for response and prayer. If you are working with Habitat for Humanity, the morning devotion is an expectation. The job supervisor either joins us at the Volunteer Center or we are invited to do this at the work site when we arrive.

> *I'm pretty certain I led my first devotional on a mission trip and I'm pretty certain several other youth led a devotion for the first time on a mission trip. The adults were always there to*

help with ideas but they always encouraged us to simply share something with the group that was important or meaningful to us. So many devotionals started with just a song or short scripture passage. Most lasted longer than expected by the youth. Tears were sometimes shed, apologies offered, and wounds healed. One recollection I have from the devotionals was the feeling that I wasn't alone. I often realized I wasn't the only one who felt a certain way or believed what I believed. Our daily devotionals were a reminder of why we were there and who we were called to be. Our adult sponsors encouraged us to use our own brains, ask questions, be respectful of others, and listen to what others had to say. There was no better way to begin a day of hard work than by coming together first thing in the morning to focus on our faith.

SETH: four high school, one college trip, 1995 to 2003; adult 2004

EVENING WORSHIP/BIBLE STUDY

The evening worship/Bible study time has initiated more rich discussion than I could ever have imagined. The faith conversations sometimes continue in smaller groups after we are done. In the spring before a trip I develop a booklet as our guide for those evening studies *(See two samples—Resources 1 and 2 in the Resource Section)*. Your planning team chooses a theme for the Worship/Bible study booklet, whether it is an expansion of the annual theme for the year for the youth group and/or the congregation, or a theme based on the location of the trip ("Down to the River" for one of our Mississippi trips or "I Lift Up My Eyes to the Hills" for a trip to Taos, NM). Another option is to expand the theme from a recent presbytery or synod youth conference.

Some years music has played a part in our worship times, but that is a weak spot of mine since I am not musical. I had to rely on CDs but now iPods would work great if all are able to hear. Each session has questions for reflection based on the Bible passage or the theme. Two to three good questions are plenty. Included is a suggested action for individuals or the group to consider doing and a space for keeping journals for the handful who enjoy that type of activity.

DRAWING NAMES FOR PRAYER

I take an envelope with strips of folded paper. Each strip has the name of one participant and all are included—youth and adults. After or during the evening worship/Bible study time on the first night, the envelope is passed around and each person draws a name. Invite them to pray for their person in secret during the week, taking note if that person is having a struggle either on the job site or with another person, or if the person is excited about discovering a new skill. Then the prayers are tailored to the needs of that person. On the last night after worship, the names are revealed and each individual summarizes their prayers and observations regarding their person. It is a very powerful time as heartfelt observations are made and prayers are shared.

Even a goof-up can turn into a moment of grace. The first year we did this activity, one of the boys drew a name, then promptly forgot about praying for the person, and even forgot whose name had been on the slip of paper. On Friday night, after one person told how they had prayed for "Oliver," it became "Oliver's" turn to share. With a totally embarrassed and sheepish grin, he confessed to having lost the name. He stated that as soon as the whole group had spoken, he would know who was left out and that he was going to give that person the biggest hug in the world and apologize. "Oliver" was teased but he followed through on his promise of a hug, the girl forgave him with laughter, and the adults stepped in to affirm Oliver for the smooth way he handled the situation. Of course, the following year Oliver was teased when names were drawn the first night and the group relived the story, but once again there was an opportunity for me to brag in front of the group about how well he had handled the situation the year before.

TEACHABLE MOMENTS

Take advantage of experiences to comment on or ask questions. If possible, ask the youth to reflect on different experiences soon after they happen. Again, I use Habitat for Humanity as an example.

- Where did you see/feel God at work today?

- How was it to work alongside the home recipient today?

- What impressed you the most at the Civil Rights Museum? At the pot luck community supper? At the closing dedication service?

- How are the demonstrations of deep faith of the Habitat neighbors in Ferrell-Sherard different from our own?

Pick up on their comments to expand their thinking, but do it without being critical or authoritarian. The typical "tell me more about that" is a great open-ended way to help them explore their thoughts a little more. I suggest we help the youth (and adults!) move beyond predictable and dead-end comments like, "I am doing this because it makes me feel so good" or "It makes me realize how blessed I am." Instead, ask them what will motivate them to continue doing good when they return home.

6

Organizing the Mission Trip:
THE PRACTICAL STUFF

The bulk of this chapter is devoted to outlining the main things to prepare over the course of the year before a mission trip. I like to think of this process as "organizing for spontaneity," a paradox that reflects the reality that the more details that can be taken care of ahead of time, the more the leaders are free to enjoy "being in the moment" with the youth. Indeed, the serendipitous moments are often those that we come to cherish the most, so don't plan so tightly that the Holy Spirit has no room to work within the group. Planning for the mission trip should begin one year prior to leaving on the journey.

If you feel the need for requirements regarding participation on the trips, establish them early.

I am aware of many youth groups that require a certain degree of participation in events in the life of the church in order for a student to be allowed to go on the trip. I have always chosen to err on the side of grace, and encourage but not require participation in fundraisers, which for us has been an annual garage sale. The youth know that they and their parents are expected to be involved, but exceptions exist. The date of the garage sale sometimes conflicts with mandatory school activities over which the youth has no control, but hopefully they or a parent can help the week before with sorting and pricing items.

A couple of times I have been questioned on this "loose" requirement regarding who goes as someone thinks that a particular person "does not deserve to go" because he/she has not been very involved in the youth group. My standard response AND my firm belief is to ask: "What if God has nudged him/her to come with us?" These trips can be transformative and can be the catalyst for greater involvement.

We are people of grace, not works. A requirement to attend a particular percentage of worship services or youth fellowship events or church school seems to counter the notion of grace.

Sometimes one of our youth wants to bring a friend. That is allowed if our numbers permit. The only stipulation is that the friend should get to know us by coming to an event or two as well as help with the garage sale. I have discovered that problems are more likely to arise with a youth who does not know any of the adults or have a sense of respect for us and our guidance. Thus, it is helpful to get to know them a little bit prior to the trip.

What follows is an outline of the most important things to prepare over the course of the year before a mission trip.

PLANNING AHEAD: ONE YEAR OUT

Form a Planning Team

Don't try to do it all yourself. Not only will it drive you crazy, but putting together a team gives participants an early investment in the success of the trip.

We have a Youth Ministry Council composed of all youth sponsors and youth representatives from each grade from seventh through twelfth. This becomes our "Planning Team." Team members make the important decisions and carry out necessary tasks.

Deciding What to Do and Where to Go

Determine what kind of work you want to do that matches the gifts and abilities of your group, then seek an agency and location that offer that. Some groups may enjoy leading a Vacation Church School with children in the visited area. Others want to help build a home or work with a shelter for the homeless. Above all, make sure the work is meaningful. One church went to the same location in Mexico two years in a row. It turned out that little work was available and the youth were asked to paint wooden folding chairs which they did not mind doing until they returned the following year and were asked to re-paint the same chairs. The youth as a group felt they wanted to do something more significant in the future.

In choosing a place to go, our rule of thumb has been a practical one. It costs a lot to fly, so we have looked for places within a day's drive. If we needed more capacity than our church van and a U-Haul trailer, we rented vans. Even our two trips to the Mexico border were only a one-day drive away. My personal goal has been for the youth to experience a different culture from our own. In recent years we have alternated trips between the Mississippi Delta, currently Jonestown Habitat, and Taos Habitat in New Mexico.

Bias Alert and New Reality: My first experience with Habitat for Humanity sold me on that organization, and twenty-six of the twenty-nine high school and college trips have been to work with them. Habitat is an organization with Christian roots that respects the dignity and value of the home recipients. There are affiliates in most areas of the country and a work format that is already in place with a job supervisor. The reality is that in the past couple of years, new age restrictions regarding construction and the use of power tools have been put in place. If you want to explore opportunities with Habitat, check with the local affiliate to make sure that your fifteen and sixteen year-olds will have something significant to do.

Because we keep returning to the same locations every other year, I reserve the weeks we want two years ahead of time, but it is typically not necessary to do it quite that early. Reservations are best made by July or August of the year before you plan to go. Due to the desire of NorthPark's high school graduates to continue with mission trips, we added college trips a few years ago, with the college group going in mid-to-late May as soon as colleges let out and before summer jobs start, and with the high school group going as soon as graduation takes place. There are many advantages to both groups going to the same place in the same year. The college trip, which typically involves fewer young people, is like a trial run before the high school trip.

To find locations for service trips, check with your presbytery or local denominational governing body for suggestions or call other churches to see where they have gone. Perhaps someone in your congregation has connections with a particular agency. The following suggestions are just the tip of the iceberg. Contact Habitat for Humanity headquarters for locations/affiliates (www.habitat.org) or contact your own denominational headquarters. For the Presbyterian Church (USA), go to gamc.pcusa.org/ministries/missiontrips/find-mission-trips-sites/ or gamc.pcusa.org/ministries/pda/who-we-are/ and click "work teams." Another agency is Door Network at doornetwork.org, which works with urban homeless persons in several cities across the U.S. If you want to help rebuild homes in the New Orleans area, which is still struggling after Hurricane Katrina, go to www.projecthomecoming.net/summer-youth-trips. This organization is working in partnership with Presbyterian Disaster Assistance and offers structured activities for worship, discussion, and hands-on mission.

Before contacting a place or agency, have an idea of how many participants you likely will bring. Some locations cannot accommodate groups larger than twenty-four or so. If your group is really small, do not be discouraged. Five or six youth and a couple of adults make a viable group, or consider inviting one or two other congregations to go with you. Also ask about age limitations as many agencies will not take middle-school youth. The middle-schoolers at NorthPark have found alternative places to serve for a shorter length of time, such as three days at Mission 911 in Corpus Christi, Texas or visiting Heifer Ranch in Perryville, Arkansas.

Accommodations

Habitat has Volunteer Centers in many locations. If not, or if using another organization, inquire about places to stay. As you investigate the possibilities, keep in mind that a gathering space for evening fellowship, study, and games is critical. Motels do not have the space for these important *community building* activities. It is advisable to make these reservations at the same time you reserve dates with an agency. Another option is to check with churches near the work site that have showers, a kitchen, and a gathering space as you can always take cots or bedrolls for sleeping on the floor of classrooms.

Inconvenience is part of the experience! When we went to work with Habitat in Nashville in 1988, we slept on the floor of a church and showered at the YMCA down the street. On our first trip to the Mississippi Delta to work in Coahoma, there was no volunteer center yet, so we stayed in the empty dorm of a junior college where we painted dorm rooms in exchange for accommodation. We were offered a motel in Clarksdale, but the other adults and I decided the experience would be a richer one by staying where we did.

Questions to ask of agencies/ministries:
- How many volunteers can they accommodate?
- Are there any age restrictions?
- What type of work can you expect?
- Do they provide a job supervisor?
- Does your crew need any construction expertise?

- What accommodations are available in the area?
- What is the cost for the accommodations?
- What are the bathroom facilities like? Number of showers?
- Are there kitchen facilities to prepare your own meals?
- Will there be any other groups staying there and sharing the facilities with you?
- Will they provide an orientation session? When and where?
- What is the typical work schedule?
- Will there be a free day or free afternoon to sight see?
- Is there an expectation of a donation for materials? If so, how much?
- Are there any other costs required?
- Are there any other expectations of the youth and/or leaders?
- What tools should you bring?
- What clothing do they recommend?
- Is it best to bring your own lunches to the worksite or is there time to return to your accommodations to eat lunch?
- What papers and inoculations are needed if working outside the U.S.?

PLANNING AHEAD: SIX MONTHS OUT
Budget

Create a preliminary budget, taking into consideration the fees required by the agency, accommodations, food, gas, etc. (*See "Budget Worksheet" —Resource 3 in Resource Section*). Then estimate the number of people you hope to take with you and figure the cost per person. It is important for the participants to make a financial commitment so they are invested in the trip, but it is also important to keep the cost affordable for the youth. No one should be excluded because of the cost. For that reason, we always offer scholarships if that is needed. Not only did we have at least one youth a year utilize the scholarship offer, we once flew a college student to and from his new home state so he could join us on a college trip. It was important to keep him connected.

To keep the cost to each individual at a reasonable level, "guesstimate" how much you need to raise via fundraisers so you can begin to figure what each participant will need to pay. Consider other sources for income as well. Does your congregation have a mission committee or other council with a budget from whom you might seek funds?

Our trips average anywhere from $295 to $450 per person, and each year we charged each youth anywhere from $150 to $200, depending upon the anticipated cost and the results of fundraisers. The fee for sponsors is paid through our fundraisers as they are taking vacation time to go and in some cases losing income to be gone for a week.

Start Publicity

At least by January, put out your first announcements of the summer trip or trips so youth and adults can place the dates on their calendars. Let them know that the cost to them will depend upon the success of the fundraisers, but you hope to keep it between $150 and $200. The fundraisers often take place before some of the youth know if they can go or not, but the fundraisers can involve all the youth as an activity for the whole group. Lots of fellowship takes place at our garage sales with the preparations and pricing that goes on for days before the event, so all are encouraged to participate.

PLANNING AHEAD: FIVE MONTHS OUT
Schedule Commissioning of Mission Trip Participants

Work with the pastor and staff to set a date for commissioning the participants during worship a week or two prior to departure. Our worship calendar fills up with additional things, so the sooner this can get on the calendar, the better. Not only does such a "sending out" reinforce for the youth and sponsors the importance of living out the biblical mandate to serve others, but it raises the awareness of the congregation as to the commitment the young people are making and invites the congregation to participate in the trip through prayer. It is an affirmation of discipleship to see the group stand before the congregation and accept the charge of serving on behalf of the church.

PLANNING AHEAD: FOUR MONTHS OUT
Fundraising and Planning for "Thank-Yous"

Rather than hold ten bake sales and twelve car washes, I prefer two solid fundraisers, which normally meets our needs, in addition to the $150 to $200 we charge the youth. If you are Presbyterian, get session approval early for the fundraisers. A garage sale every spring has become a tradition now at NorthPark, with church members saving items throughout the year for the sale. This event raises between $4,000 and $8,000 each year.

Our other fundraiser is the sale of "Habitat Stock Certificates" (Stock Certificate—Resource 4 in the Resource Section). For three Sundays in a row, youth are in the narthex taking donations in any amount. In announcements, we emphasize how much money we still need to raise for trip expenses and for the materials donation per person to Habitat. The donor records their name and physical address on a sheet of paper from which address labels are made prior to the trips. Mid-week during the trip, we purchase postcards and youth write thank-yous on the cards. These we mail to the "Habitat Stockholders" to express our gratitude for their support. Stockholders receive three postcards each if we have a middle school, high school, and college trip, as each group sends their thanks. Church members have told me that the postcard is a highlight every year and that it inspires them to give again the following year. Even if you are not working with Habitat, you can ask your congregants to make donations to purchase "Mission Trip Stock Certificates."

Lining Up Adult Sponsors

Begin firming up adult sponsors by February. It is helpful to have one adult per five to seven youth. Because we have done this for so many years and the kids look forward to it even before they reach youth group age, we have had very few discipline issues and therefore have not needed a great number of sponsors. The main issue for me is to have at least two adult drivers per van. Often we have more adults who want to go than we have space. The first shot at participating goes to our regular youth sponsors as the youth already have strong relationships with them.

If more adults are needed, ask the youth to name adults they would like on the trip. It is rare that someone turns down that kind of special request. We also go through the Mission Committee for recommendations or invite a parent with the permission of their own teen. Never do I put out a blanket invitation to the whole congregation as we this might yield a volunteer who is not the most helpful when it comes to relating to youth. More is said about the importance of the role of the adults in Chapter 2.

All adults must submit to a background check as mandated by our church's Child Protection Policy. Anyone who works in any capacity with children under 18 at NorthPark is required to fill out a form to allow this. Chapter 2 offers information on formulating such a policy.

In early May, I meet with the adult sponsors of the trips to discuss plans, work details, map of driving route, anticipated issues, expectations of the sponsors, etc. If the middle school trip is to a different location than the high school and college trips, a separate meeting takes place with the middle school trip sponsors (See "Final meeting with adult sponsors" for more details.)

PLANNING AHEAD: THREE MONTHS OUT

Headcount and Budget

By now, you should have a good idea of the approximate number of youth going and the number of adults required.

Re-examine the budget in light of these approximate numbers and adjust accordingly.

What do you do if demand exceeds available spaces? Three months' lead time gives you a chance to attempt some juggling. Gratefully, we have been able to stretch our reservations by one or two with Habitat if it was needed, so we have never had to leave anyone behind.

If numbers are an issue, perhaps another location or project needs to be found in order to include everyone who wants to go. If a decision has to be made to limit those who are interested, it would be a concern for a Youth Ministry Council (or some such group) to decide the criteria for prioritizing the youth. In that case, involvement during the year could be a guideline. We find including as many as desire to go to be the optimum position.

Transportation

Once you have an idea of how many are going on the trip, determine how many vehicles you will need and either rent vans or make necessary arrangements depending upon your numbers. We also rent a 5 x 8' trailer from U-Haul for luggage, tools, drinks and food, coolers, box fans, etc.

Always check to see if your church's tax exempt status will be honored. Some rental places do and some don't.

**Note: take copies of your church's tax exempt status form with you on the trip as you might have occasion to need it (for example, if the vehicle unexpectedly needs a new tire or if motel rooms are used on the trip home).

Plan Side Trips Ahead of Time if Reservations are Required

- Motel reservations going or returning, if needed.
- Rafting is a favorite "day off" activity when we go to Taos, NM. Reservations have to be made a couple of months out , and a deposit and waivers sent in.
- Trips to a place like the Civil Rights Museum in Memphis might need reservations ahead of time if the group is large. Also check with your mission agency contact person or Habitat contact as they might advise you about where discounts are offered to mission trip groups.
- One tradition of ours is to eat BBQ at the Rendezvous in Memphis on our free afternoon there. Reservations need to be made at least two days ahead for a group of our size.

PLANNING AHEAD: TWO MONTHS OUT

Worship/Bible Study Booklets

Preparations for our evening Bible study booklets begins in April as we settle on a theme and begin developing the brief evening discussion times. Though I have consulted with youth from our Youth Ministry Council regarding ideas for the theme and booklet, I have found that the end of the school year is not a great time for them to do the actual work. Perhaps you can develop a better schedule to allow for their rich input. More on this item is found in Chapter 5 and a sample of two of our booklets is in the *Resource Section—Resources 1 and 2.*

Get the Individual Paperwork in Order

All participants are required to sign a Covenant of Community and have a Notarized Medical Release form on file to take on the trips. The Covenant is a reminder of expectations regarding behavior and dress. At our orientation session with the parents and youth, we review the Covenant and reiterate that parents will be responsible for getting their teen home in the case of a major infraction. Gratefully, that never had to happen. Part of the Covenant has to do with modest clothing, so I suggest taking along a couple of over-sized t-shirts for the girls whose tops do not cover enough skin or for guys/girls whose shirts have an inappropriate message on them.

Twice we did have to take a youth to the Emergency Room, so having the Medical Release form is important. We keep a file of the Release

Forms, which are good throughout their career as youth at the church, but newcomers need to fill one out in order to go on the trip. Samples of both the Covenant, *Resource 5*, and Release, *Resource 6* are in the *Resource Section*.

PLANNING AHEAD: ONE MONTH OUT

Final Flyer

By early May, make sure all participants receive information on details regarding the trip, the cost to them, the commissioning date at worship before the congregation, departure time, what to bring, and the date of the orientation session with youth, sponsors, and parents of youth who are going.

Final Details

- **Get Final information.** Contact your mission trip locations and housing arrangements for final information on the work to be done by your group, supplies and tools to bring, confirmation of payment amounts remaining, etc.

- **Finalize finances.** Figure all finances for all mission trips and submit the requests to the church's financial person—checks to Habitat, checks for housing, and cash for gas, food, etc. Does your church have a credit card you can use on the trip or will you have to pay in cash?

- **Names for prayer.** Prepare an envelope with names of participants to be drawn for prayer during the week (from Chapter 5).

- **Affirmation cards.** Prepare the treasured affirmation cards ahead of time. The benefit of these cards is explained in Chapter 2.

  > Sets of name labels for each participant are needed. Make a set for each person going on the trip plus one; e.g., if 25 people are going, make 26 sets of labels.

  > One label goes on the outside of a Ziploc baggie for each person.

  > Inside the baggie are 4 x 6" cards, one for each participant except the one whose name is on the baggie. Each card will have a label for each of the other participants.

  > The baggies with cards inside are passed out on the second night of the trip so that youth and adults can begin to formulate notes to the others as the week progresses.

> Instructions: Begin to write a personal note to each one in the group, recording funny moments, powerful moments of work shared or insights gained about the other.

> Towards the end of the week, place 5 x 7" envelopes in a central location, each with the final name label so the completed affirmation cards can be put inside.

> These envelopes are distributed on the morning we return home. Every person should have a personal note for and from each of the other participants.

> The organization of these materials can be delegated but it will be a huge advantage to have them prepared ahead of time.

- **Evening worship/Bible study.** Complete copies of the evening worship/Bible study time for each participant. Take a couple of extras as someone will misplace theirs even though they are to put their name in them the first night.

- **Chores Chart.** Wherever you stay, chores will need to be done. Depending upon the number of youth going, each teen will be assigned a chore at least twice during your stay. In order to save time after your arrival and to avoid friends clamoring to sign up with their own friends, fill in the Chores Chart (*Resource 7 in the Resource Section*) before the trip and post it in the kitchen on the refrigerator or other highly visible spot. It is intentional that I pair up those who are not best friends, and I try to make sure each youth has two or three different chores with two or three different partners. No chart is needed with the college group as they more readily pitch in and work together.

- **Mosquitoes.** If you are going to a place that has mosquitoes, vitamin B1 taken three times a day starting three weeks ahead of time wards off mosquito bites for most people. A pharmacist parent told me about this and it works. This will need to be communicated a month out to those going.

- **Skills session?** Do you need to plan for a "skills" session before the trip? If you are building and have a lot of new young people, it might help to have a learning time before the trip with a place to teach them to hammer, to saw, etc.

Final Meeting with the Adult Sponsors

Conveying expectations and responsibilities to the adult team is very important to get everyone on the same page, and to assure those who do not work on a regular basis with the teens that they have the same "authority" as regular sponsors to encourage cooperation or intervene if a problem occurs. This is the time to determine who will pick up the rental van and U-Haul trailer, who has access to walkie-talkies, and who will shop for supplies ahead of departure. You can exchange cell phone numbers, discuss the travel route, go over the work week schedule, etc. Suggested items to be discussed at this meeting are *Resource 8* in the *Resource Section*.

Each sponsor is given a list of the participants and contact numbers as well as a "day-by-day" schedule (*Resource 9 in the Resource Section*) of what to anticipate and plan for. Clear communication of information is a huge deal as I did not want to be the keeper of all the details or viewed as The Expert. These trips are a partnership effort.

PLANNING AHEAD: TWO WEEKS OUT

Orientation Session with Final Information for Youth, Sponsors, and Parents

I cannot stress enough the importance of preparing the youth for the trip in terms of exploring God's call to help others. Because NorthPark Presbyterian Church has a culture of service and mission, which happens in many ways throughout the year, we usually do not have a formal teaching/learning time prior to the trip. Rather, our frequent service projects reinforce for youth and others the notion of servanthood. If this is not the case in your congregation or group, there are resources available to prepare your youth for their trip in terms of understanding why you are doing this.

One such resource to prompt conversation is entitled *Serving Others,* an online study from www.thethoughtfulchristian.org. Click "Downloadable Studies," the "Youth" link, then click "Living Your Faith." This study is among those listed.

A book that offers adult sponsors some ways to help the youth connect faith and action, both before and during the trip, is *Mission Trips That Matter* by Don C. Richter, published by Upper Room.

This orientation is the time to pass out any final information, collect money and forms, go over the covenant of community, reiterate what to bring, clarify expectations while traveling and while at the trip location, answer any questions, and to ask for volunteers to bring needed items and for youth to sign up for devotions. A suggested format for this meeting is *Resource 10* in the *Resource Section.*

Electronic Devices

One issue facing all trips these days is what to do about the use of cell phones, iPods, and other electronic devices, which are such an important part of the teens' lives. Each of you will need to come to an agreement regarding this, whether it is to tell the youth to leave all such items at home or to restrict their use. I prefer the latter primarily because our travel time tends to be ten to eleven hours in the vans. We let our youth have their devices in the vans with the understanding that when information needs to be announced or decisions made, they are to set them aside. Our experience is that after a while, human contact is more fun for the young people than staying isolated on their devices, though many times two or three will play a game together on them. Once we arrive at our destination, the devices are put into a plastic box for the duration of our time there, with the exception of half an hour between dinner and Bible study each night when youth can call home to check in.

First Meal

Another important item at the orientation is to solicit volunteers to prepare the Taco meat for the first meal after our first day of work. It became a tradition to have Taco Salad (*recipe is Resource 12 in the Resource Section*). It is a hearty meal that is adaptable both to picky eaters and to vegetarians. Most of the ingredients are purchased on our first grocery store trip at the site location, but the meat is cooked ahead of time by the teens or their parents, then brought in frozen form the morning we depart and placed in coolers. Browning the meat, draining the grease, and cooking with the Taco seasonings is the most time-consuming part of the meal, so to have it prepared ahead of time with only a need to heat it up is a gigantic help.

PLANNING AHEAD: THE WEEK BEFORE THE TRIP

- **Cash.** Make a trip to your church's bank to cash a check made out to you for money needed on the trip (unless your church has a credit card).

- **Shop for supplies to take with you.** Go to SAMs, Costco, or another discount store for an initial supply of cases of water and Gatorade, snacks, cereal, lunch items (sandwich baggies, giant Ziploc baggies for protecting sandwiches in coolers at work site, individual bags of chips, cookies, dried fruit) napkins and other paper products—bowls for cereal, plates for supper, plastic utensils, etc. A suggested shopping list is *Resource 13* in the *Resource Section*. Note: We limit the number of sodas we take along. Water and Gatorade are much better in terms of rehydrating during work. Sodas are normally for supper only.

- **Materials to have on hand.** Gather materials and supplies to take with you, such as masking tape, scissors, Sharpies, etc. (*Suggested list is Resource 12 in the Resource Section*)

- **Room assignments if needed.** Some volunteer centers or accommodations have space for all the girls in one big room and all the guys in another. In that situation we let them choose their own beds. However, if the place we are going to stay has several small bedrooms for three or four, I usually work out tentative room assignments ahead of time so that we do not have to labor over the decision upon arrival. Normally I create a suggested room arrangement, then give it to willing youth from our Youth Council and let them hammer out a better arrangement. Nothing is ever in stone if the young people want to make a change once we arrive, but it saves a huge amount of negotiating upon arrival and avoids hurt feelings to have a plan in place. I only had to experience one teen in tears at being left out as people rushed to rooms to prompt me to do it differently if space was going to be an issue. With the college groups I never make room assignments.

DAY BY DAY ON THE TRIP

Your schedule will be dictated by travel time, the work you will be doing, number of days on the work site, the free afternoon or day that you will have, etc. In the *Resource Section* is a typical day-by-day format (*Resource 9*) that I found helpful for our trips. The other adults had a copy as well. Again, this is not to structure activities tightly but rather to avoid having something fall through the cracks.

AFTER THE TRIP

There are many ways to help the youth and adults reflect on the trip. As we travel home, each van has a clipboard with notebook paper on it and a pencil. The youth are invited to jot down their impressions on the trip, which are then published in the church's newsletter. This is one way to begin the process of debriefing and noting the significance of their experience.

Back in the days of actual photos, we would gather at the church about a week after the trip when everyone had had a chance to get their film developed, and they would create posters of the trip to put up in the church. We would reminisce and reflect as we worked together.

A few weeks after the trips, we have a congregational lunch on a Sunday after worship to thank the congregation for their support and to share with them what was accomplished. Though I have adults help me to edit the video footage taken on the trips, the middle schoolers sometimes create their own digital slide show of where they went. It is important to let the congregation see what the young people did and listen to them describe the work, their impressions, and the impact it had on them. The opportunity to share with the congregation cements the importance of what they did and gives them an opportunity to receive affirmations from the church. A group photo is taken on each trip, later enlarged and displayed for all to see. The education wing at NorthPark has a series of 8x10s and 11x16s on its walls.

If we are aware of specific needs of a recipient family with whom we work, we give an item or gift card to them at the end of the trip or send it upon our return or at Christmas. This is always a youth group decision if we have funds left over.

For the trips to have a transformative influence, introspection within oneself and within the group needs to happen. In addition to the ideas above, there are resources to help you in that process. A helpful one-session study is *That Mission Trip Was Fun! Now What?* This is an online resource from www.thethoughtfulchristian.org. Click "Downloadable Studies," the "Youth" link, then click *"Living Your Faith."* Scroll down to this study.

In closing, may you find the ideas presented in this book to be helpful and the stories to be inspiring. May you experience new life along with Lazarus as you embark on a new journey through mission trips or continue your planning of such trips in new ways. Never would I have dreamed that God had such richness in store for me and the 197 youth and adults who have accompanied me on the 29 trips. Their witness to Christ's love as well as that of the countless wonderful people at the locations to which we traveled has unbound me and transformed me as we served as partners in Christ's service. Thanks be to God.

RESOURCES

*To access these resources as Word documents in order to adapt them for your own use, go to www.unboundmissiontrips.com, click on the tab for **RESOURCES** and log in with the user name: **leader** and the password: **unbound**. All are lower case.*

Salt and Light

[ADD NAME OF YOUR CHURCH, DESTINATION OF MISSION TRIP, AND DATE]

WORSHIP BOOK

NAME

Welcome to Mission Trip [ADD YEAR]

MISSION WEEK PRAYER

I Tremble on the Edge of a Maybe

O God of beginnings, as your Spirit moved
over the face of the deep
on the first day of creation,
move with me now in my time of beginnings,
when the air is rain-washed, the bloom is on the bush,
and the world seems fresh
and full of possibilities
and I feel ready and full.

I tremble on the edge of a maybe,
a first time, a new thing, a tentative start,
and the wonder of it lays its finger on my lips.

In silence, Lord, I share now my eagerness
and my uneasiness about this something different
I would be or do;
and I listen for your leading
to help me separate the light from the darkness
in the change I seek to shape
and which is shaping me.

Amen

*Taken from Guerrillas of Grace: Prayers for the Battle by Ted Loder,
Copyright 1984 by Ted Loder. Used by permission of Augsburg Fortress
Publishers. www.augsburgfortress.org*

Trip Participants

Students
(list names)

Adults
(list names)

Daily Schedule in [ADD LOCATION]

7:00 am	WAKE UP!
7:00 am	Breakfast
7:45 am	Breakfast crew clean-up
8:00 am	Morning devotions
	Work day instructions
8:30 am	On the job site
Noon	Lunch
4:30 pm	End of work day,
	clean up at job site
4:45 pm	Showers, relax
6:00 pm	Supper
7:00 pm	Evening devotions
7:30 pm	Recreation/games/free time/
	Walmart?
11:30 pm	Quiet hours begin: in rooms,
	lights out!

We are Called to be Salt and Light

DAY 1

Opening thoughts: God calls us to reflect his light as we serve in his world and respond to the needs of others. We can be self-centered or God-centered as we go about doing his work.

Opening prayer (in unison):
We come before you tonight, Lord, feeling weary with travel, excited to be in this place, and a little apprehensive as we anticipate the days ahead of us. Give us your peace and sense of purpose as we settle into a routine for the week. In Jesus' name we pray. Amen.

Scripture reading: John 11:38-44

Thoughts and questions for reflection: Jesus demonstrated his power by resurrecting Lazarus and bringing him out of the darkness of death into the light. After such a demonstration of power, he could have just called out for the grave cloths to disappear. Instead, he invited the people to unwrap Lazarus.

- What did Jesus mean by the command to unbind Lazarus and let him go?
- If this is an image of what we are to do for one another, what are some things that bind us up and prevent us from being all that God wants us to be?

JOURNAL

Write down inside the candle how you can unbind your [ADD YOUR CHURCH NAME] friends and how you can unbind the people of this Mississippi community.

• What are some things that bind up the people in [LOCATION] that prevent them from being all that God intends them to be?

• What role can we play this week to unbind them?

Remember this is a two-way process, so be open to the ways that the people of [INSERT LOCATION] will unbind you.

Reaching out: Be intentional this week in looking for ways to unbind your [ADD YOUR CHURCH NAME] friends (as well as the people of this [ADD PLACE NAME] community) as you serve God together.

• How can you help them become more what God intends for them to be?

One way we can do that in a quiet way is through prayer. Draw a name from the envelope. Keep the name a secret, but pray all week for this person. At the end of the week, we will share whose name each of us drew.

Closing prayer:

Leader: Jesus Christ is the light of the world.

People: The light that no darkness can overcome.

Leader: Stay with us, Lord, for it is evening,

People: And the day is almost over.

Leader: Give us a good night's rest and a sense of purposefulness for tomorrow.

All: Give us sensitive hearts to see how we can help each other become all we can. Amen.

We are Called to be Salt and Light

DAY 2

Opening thoughts: The community of faith is charged to be salt to the world. Part of what this means is that what we do and say is to be relevant to our own lives and to the lives of others.

Opening prayer (in unison):
Gracious God, our first day of work has been tiring and hot. We have met new people and done new things. In spite of our fatigue, you have refreshed us with food and with the company of one another. Even in our weariness, let us be salt and light to one another and the people of this [ADD MIS-SION LOCATION] community. In Jesus' name we pray. Amen

Scripture reading: Matthew 5:13

Thoughts and questions for reflection:
Salt was used for many things in Bible times:

- For seasoning food: a pinch of salt is added to food to provide zest and enhance flavor.

- As a preservative: without refrigeration, people salted meat to preserve it. Christians are called to be preserving agents in a world that is sometimes bent on destruction.

- For healing: in Bible times, wounds were treated with salt. It hurt but was needed to promote healing.

- Salt makes people thirsty. Our presence is intended by God to make the people around us thirst for the presence of God, for what they see in us.

- Name someone you know and tell how they have demonstrated one of these qualities of salt.

Salt can lose its flavor through exposure to damaging conditions such as moisture or getting mixed in with something else like sand.

- Do you think the world needs or wants the "salt" that Christians have to offer? Why or why not?

- What are some reasons that disciples can fail to add zest to the life of the community of faith or fail to preserve the love of God around others?

Closing prayer:

Leader: Colossians 4:6 says, "Let your speech always be gracious, seasoned with salt, so that you may know how you ought to answer everyone."

People: We are salt when we are both truth and grace to a world filled with promises that are not "worth their salt."

Leader: As we live together and work together, may we enrich the lives of others with our "saltiness."

All: May we remain distinctive in our life style and give glory to God rather than blend in with the rest of the world. Amen.

We are Called to be Salt and Light

DAY 3

Opening thoughts: When Jesus said, "I am the light of the world" and commanded that his disciples be light to the world, he was demanding that we be like him. Jesus knew that we could not kindle our own light. He meant that we are to shine with the reflection of his light.

Opening prayer (in unison):
We give you thanks, God, for safe travels this afternoon and a fun break for the afternoon. Help us to focus on what you would have us learn from our experiences and from your Word. Amen.

Scripture reading: Matthew 5:14-15

Thoughts and questions for reflection:

Without the light of the sun, we cannot live. Nothing grows, nothing thrives, and nothing survives without light. Light also illumines and unveils. As the Light of the World, Jesus brings spiritual sight to a blind world in darkness. We are called to bring spiritual light into the dark corners around us by living a life that is pleasing to God.

JOURNAL

How do you provide spice, zest, and flavor to the situations around you? Write your response inside the candle.

JOURNAL

Think of ways that you can let your faith be visible and not hidden, even this week as we are together. Write them inside your candle.

- How can we do that? How can we make our faith visible to others?

- Are you prepared for people to be watching the way you live? Why or why not?

- We are challenged to expose evil. Name one situation where you have shed light in the darkness or you have seen someone else shine light in the darkness.

- Has a Christian friend ever said, "I will not be a part of that"?

- What makes that hard to do?

Closing prayer (in unison):

Help us, O God, to be a light to those near and far. Lead us in the ways of service that will bless others. Help us fall asleep with you in our hearts and minds as we seek ways to be your light in the world. In Jesus' name. Amen.

We are Called to be Salt and Light

DAY 4

Opening thoughts: A light is something that is supposed to be seen. A light is something that makes the way more clear to others. It serves no purpose if it is hidden.

Opening prayer (in unison):

You are the light of the world, O Christ, yet sometimes we do not reflect that light. You have called us to be salt, but often our lives are bland and inspire no one. Forgive us for these times, set us right, and renew us by your Spirit. In Jesus' name. Amen.

Scripture reading: Matthew 5:14–15

Thoughts and questions for reflection:

- Is there such a thing as a "closet" Christian? A secret Christian? Why or why not?

- Why is it easy to remain silent when others are planning something hurtful or inappropriate?

- When is your light the strongest?

- What crowds out your light and makes it shine weakly or not at all?

Closing prayer:

Leader: God, sometimes it feels like we spend a lot of time stumbling around in the dark.

People: Light the path, God.

Leader: There are so many choices, so many people who want just a little piece of our time.

People: Light the path, God.

Leader: There are so many things that take up our time, so many ways to mess up our lives.

People: Light the path, God.

Leader: The dark is a scary place, but we are not alone. You are with us, God.

People: Light the path, God.

Leader: We may not know where we are going, but we will trust you, God. We will believe in your light.

People: Light the path, God. Amen.

We are Called to be Salt and Light

DAY 5

Opening thoughts: Other people should be able to see our good deeds, but these deeds should draw attention to God, not to us. It has been said that the Christian does not think of what he/she has done, but of what God has enabled and empowered him/her to do.

Opening prayer (in unison):

Gracious and loving God, your light never fades. Show us how to keep your light shining in our lives. In your holy name. Amen.

Scripture reading: Matthew 5:16

Thoughts and questions for reflection:

- Reveal to one another whose name you drew for prayer and how that made a difference in your week.
- This week, how have you been unbound, like Lazarus, to become more who God intends you to be?
- What examples of light have the people of [your mission location] been for us?

JOURNAL

List some of the things that prevent you from reflecting Christ's light.

What can you do to change that?

Closing prayer:

Leader: We have come together this week to serve, to be community, to receive light and be light.

People: We pray our actions and words have been blessings to others, both in our group and among the people we came to serve.

Leader: May we see the world more clearly now after a week of trying faithfully to live out your call.

All: May we continue to be windows through which the world can know of your light and your love. May all we do glorify you. Amen.

JOURNAL

List ways you have been set free this week, whether it is a new thing you have learned about yourself or something positive that someone said to you.

List some ways you helped unbind someone else so they can be all God intends them to be.

Thin Places
Catching Glimpses of God

[ADD NAME OF YOUR CHURCH, DESTINATION OF MISSION TRIP, AND DATE]

WOSHIP BOOK

NAME

Trip Participants

Students

(list names)

Adults

(list names)

WELCOME TO MISSION TRIP 20--!

Thin Places

where we sense the presence of God;

where we catch glimpses of God;

where we find God in the ordinary events of life, love, eating, working, playing;

where we find holiness in every moment.

A symbol of Celtic Christianity is the circle to represent the connectedness of all things. The Celtic cross has a circle at its center.

Thin Places

DAY 1

Main idea: LIGHT REVEALS "THIN PLACES" WHERE WE CAN CATCH GLIMPSES OF GOD

Christians are aware that in one sense there is a veil between us and God that tends to separate us. God is omniscient and omnipresent and holy and "other," yet we also know that God is close, caring for us and guiding us and comforting us. How does the sacred break into the ordinary? Will we recognize it?

Opening Celtic prayer (in unison):

Lord of the unexpected, you have travelled with us as we drove today. You have gone before us to this place. We are pilgrims in life, but especially we are pilgrims this week as we journey to a new adventure in your name. Walk with us each day we are here. Surprise us on our path. Open our eyes to see your presence now and always. In Jesus' name we pray. Amen.

Scripture: John 1:1-5; 8:12

Jesus said "I AM the Light of the World"

Daily Schedule in [ADD DESTINATION, AND SCHEDULE BELOW]

7:00 am	Up and at 'em
	Breakfast
7:45 am	Breakfast crew clean-up
8:00 am	Morning devotions
	Work day instructions
8:30 am	On the job site
Noon	Break for lunch
4:30 pm	End of work day; clean up at job site
4:45 pm	Showers, relax
6:00 pm	Supper
7:00 pm	Evening devotions/Bible study
7:30 pm	Recreation/games/free time
11:30 pm	Quiet hours begin: in rooms, lights out

Thoughts and questions for reflection:

When Moses asked God in the burning bush what he should say to the Israelites when they asked for the name of this God who sent him, God said to tell them "I AM WHO I AM." The "I am" sayings in the Gospel of John are Jesus' self-revelations.

Jesus is making a direct connection with God and identifying himself as the one in whom God is visible and made known.

- When is a time you have walked in the darkness? Have you been able to get back into the light? What did it take to do that?

- How is Jesus the "light" for you?

- What helps you to stay in the light and to be aware of God's presence?

Reaching out: Draw a name from the envelope. Keep the name a secret, but pray all week for this person. At the end of the week, we will each share whose name we drew.

Closing prayer:

Leader: Jesus Christ is the light of the world.

People: The light that no darkness can overcome.

Leader: Stay with us, Lord, for it is evening,

People: And the day is almost over.

Leader: Give us a good night's rest and a sense of purposefulness for tomorrow.

All: Give us sensitive hearts to see how we can help each other become all we can. Amen.

JOURNAL

Around and within the Celtic cross, write down your hopes and expectations of this week together.

Thin Places

DAY 2

Main idea: IN THIN PLACES WE HEAR JESUS' VOICE AND KNOW WE BELONG TO HIS FLOCK.

Opening prayer *in unison:*

Eternal God, Loving Shepherd, as we move through our week, enliven our minds, inspire our conversation, inform our decisions, and protect those we love. And should this week bring what we neither anticipate nor desire, increase our faith and decrease our pride until we know that, when we face the unexpected, we do not stand alone. Hear these prayers made in the presence and in the name of Jesus Christ our Lord. Amen.

Scripture: John 10:1-5, 11-18
    Jesus said, "I AM the Good Shepherd"

Thoughts and questions for reflection:

The Good Shepherd knows us, leads us, and lays down his life for us. Listening to Jesus' voice is a mark of faithfulness.

- Describe the relationship between the good shepherd and his sheep.
- How do you really "know" you belong to God?
- When is a time you experienced Jesus as the Good Shepherd, the one who guides and protects?
- What are some ways you "listen" for Jesus' voice?

Reaching out: Tonight and tomorrow listen for God's "voice" through the people around you. Think about ways to reach out tomorrow not just to our own group but to those we meet on our afternoon off.

Closing prayer *in unison:*

Tonight, O Lord, may we remember your mercy given so gently and generously.

Each thing we have received, from you it came.

Each thing for which we hope, from your love it will come.

Each thing we enjoy, it is of your bounty.

Each thing we ask, comes of your arranging.

Through our Lord, Jesus Christ. Amen.

Thin Places

DAY 3

Main idea: THE LORD'S SUPPER CAN BE A THIN PLACE WHERE OUR RELATIONSHIP WITH GOD IS FED AND NOURISHED.

By participating in the Lord's Supper we strengthen our relationship with Christ.

Opening prayer *(in unison)*:
Holy God, we know that those who wish to serve him must first be served by him, and

Those who wish to follow him must first be fed by him.

God intends for us to be nourished.

Christ intends to make us new. Amen.

Scripture: John 6:35-40, 56-58
Jesus said, "I AM the Bread of Life"

JOURNAL

Think about a time when you heard God's voice and responded. How did you know it was God nudging you?

JOURNAL

Celtic Christians believe that an ordinary day can become an occasion for finding God. Inside the Celtic cross, indicate where you found God today.

Thoughts and questions for reflection:

- What does Jesus mean that we, as believers, will never hunger or thirst?

- Bread smells great, is savory, filling, and satisfying. What experiences fill you and satisfy you spiritually?

- Life is more than just staying alive through food. What is necessary for life to be as God intended it to be?

Reaching out: Think about the person whose name you drew for prayer. What can you do this week, with God's help, to nourish him/her?

Closing prayer:

Leader: In deep gratitude, we give ourselves to you, gracious God.

People: Help us to live as changed people because we have shared the Living Bread and cannot remain the same.

Leader: Ask much of us, expect much from us, enable much by us, encourage many through us.

People: May we live to your glory, both as inhabitants of earth and citizens of heaven.

Amen.

Thin Places

DAY 4

Main idea: THE HOLY SPIRIT MEANS GOD'S PRESENCE DWELLS WITHIN US. THE POTENTIAL FOR THIN PLACES IS WITH US AND WITHIN US.

Opening prayer:

Leader: Breath of God, breath of life, breath of deepest yearning,

People: Come, Holy Spirit

Leader: Comforter, disturber, interpreter, enthuser,

People: Come, Holy Spirit

Leader: Heavenly friend, lamplighter, revealer of truth, midwife of change,

People: Come, Holy Spirit

All: God's Spirit is with us. Amen and amen.

Scripture: John 15:15-20, 25-27

The Holy Spirit is promised

Thoughts and questions for reflection:

The Holy Spirit will continue to make visible the presence of God in Christ. When Jesus left, we were promised the ongoing presence of God and Jesus. This is our connection with God.

- What does a counselor do? How is the Holy Spirit a counselor to us?

- Of all the promises given in this passage, which one means the most to you?

- What is the difference between the way the world gives peace and the way Jesus gives peace?

- On a scale from 1 to 10, how would you describe the level of peace in your life right now—level 1 being a low level of peace, 10 being the highest level?

Reaching out: Think of a way you can encourage a sense of peace for someone else on this trip...through a word or action...and pray they will discover a Thin Place in their lives.

Closing prayer (in unison):

May God bless us
In our sleep with rest,
In our dreams with vision,
In our waking with a calm mind,
In our soul with the friendship of the Holy Spirit,
This night and every night.
Amen.

Thin Places

DAY 5

Main idea: TO ABIDE IN CHRIST IS TO BE IN A THIN PLACE, TO BE IN GOD'S PRESENCE.

Opening prayer (in unison):

Gracious God, in gratitude, in deep gratitude for this week together, these people, this work, we give ourselves to you. When we leave, let us go out to live as changed people because we have shared in your work and been in your presence. We cannot remain the same. In Christ's name. Amen.

Scripture: John 15:1-17 **I AM the true Vine**

Thoughts and questions for reflection:

To abide means to "remain," to remain in a relationship with God and Jesus and with one another. The life of the Christian community is shaped by love, and intertwined with the abiding presence of God and Jesus. The Father's love for Jesus is mirrored in Jesus' love for his disciples. Jesus asks the community to mirror that love in their own actions. Bearing fruit means doing acts of love, a concrete sign of discipleship.

JOURNAL

Where/when did you feel the Spirit's guidance today? Write that inside the Celtic cross.

JOURNAL

List around and inside the Celtic cross the activities, people, and places that have been Thin Places for you this week.

- What is the biggest barrier for you in abiding/remaining in relationship with Christ?
- Name a time when you felt strongly connected to Christ?
- What fruits or acts of love have you witnessed this week?
- In what ways can you be a fruit-bearer, showing acts of love?

Reaching out: Tell one another who your prayer recipient has been this week.

- What has it meant to you to know someone was praying for you?

Close with a circle prayer.

Budget Worksheet

Figuring the cost of a mission trip

_____ # of students

_____ # of adults

BUDGET ITEMS

Rental: One 15-passenger van _____

Gas for vans _____

Rental: U-Haul trailer _____

Food * _____

Construction or supplies donation often required by
    Habitat ($150 per person) and other organizations

Accommodations _____

Any sight-seeing costs (museum? tour?) _____

Miscellaneous
    (postcards,stamps, photo cards, building supplies) _____

Gift cards (if interested and able)
    for job supervisor, new home owner _____

Total expenses: _____

INCOME

$_____ per youth X # of youth (less ___ on scholarship)** _____

Total Income from garage sale & Habitat "stock"
    (or other fundraisers): _____

Need to raise: _____

*Average per person for NorthPark's 2010 4-day, 5-night stay in MS = $80 on college trip and $70 on high school trip (less cost of taco meat provided by parents with first meal and dinner prepared by Habitat community on Thursday night) including eating out on Wednesday & Friday nights (one of those is pizza). Everyone pays for own meals when we are traveling to and from mission site.

**Cost to our sponsors is paid for through fundraisers

Stock Certificate

{Your church/org name} Habitat Stock Certificate

1 SHARE

ONE SHARE

The bearer, _____, is a member of a unique, caring group of individuals who realizes the importance of serving those in need. The bearer covenants with the youth of {your church/organization name} to pray for them while they are on the {year} {mission name} mission trip to {location} and will support their efforts through donations.

Covenant of Conduct

MISSION TRIP TO [ADD DESTINATION]
[INSERT NAME OF YOUR CHURCH]

I will support the rules set by the sponsors and do what they ask. I will encourage the other youth to do the same.

I agree to work to the best of my abilities and to participate with the group in the designated activities and those approved by the sponsors.

I will ask permission of the sponsors to participate in any additional activities.

I will not smoke, bring or consume alcohol or illegal drugs, and will not bring fireworks, shaving cream, or any other things to play "tricks" on others.

I will respect the property of the places where we stay, and will leave them either in the condition in which I found them or better.

I will show respect for all persons and their property. I will not insult or put anybody down.

I recognize that I have been created in the image of God and that this belief is to be reflected in my behavior and dress. Therefore, I will behave in an appropriate manner with the opposite sex and will dress modestly, avoiding T-shirts with unsuitable messages, loose pants that show underwear, tank tops, halter-tops, showing cleavage or bare midriffs, short shorts, and skirts shorter than "fingertip length."

I will honor the "lights-out" time that is established by the sponsors.

I will honor the limits to cell phone use and headphone use established by the sponsors.

I understand that if I violate any portion of this covenant, the sponsors will contact my parents and arrangements will be made for me to be sent home at my parents' expense.

I, _____, have read and agree with these stipulations.

_____   _____
Signature of youth   Date

_____   _____
Signature of parent/guardian   Date

Notarized Medical Release Form

I hereby give my child, _____, permission to participate with the [NAME OF YOUR CHURCH] youth group in their youth activities from the date I sign this form until I notify [NAME OF YOUR CHURCH] in writing that it is no longer effective. In connection with the group activities within that time frame, I hereby release and discharge [NAME OF YOUR CHURCH, TOWN, STATE], its Pastors, Directors of Christian Education, agents, employees, and designated adult sponsors of and from all liability, loss, cost, or expense of whatsoever kind of such nature which might arise by virtue of any injury to my child.

_____   _____
Signature of youth   Date

I, _____, understand that I assume all risks involved in connection with the above activities.

_____   _____
Signature of youth   Date

ALLERGIES, MEDICATIONS, OTHER MEDICAL INFORMATION

In the event my child requires medical attention of any kind, I hereby designate to any of the adult sponsors, the Pastors, or the Director of Christian Education the full power and authority to secure or receive whatever medical attention and assistance they feel is desirable or necessary for my child, including, but not limited to the power to authorize such treatment as the setting of broken bones, administration of anesthetics, or any other desirable or necessary medical or surgical procedure for my child.

_____   _____   _____
Signature of parent/guardian   Home phone   Work phone

_____   _____
Address   City/State/Zip

THE STATE OF [ADD], County of [ADD]

Before me, the undersigned authority, on this day personally appeared _____, known to me to be the person whose name is subscribed to the foregoing instrument, and acknowledged to me that he/she executed the same for the purposes and consideration therein expressed.

Given under my hand and seal of office on   _____

                                                             _____
                                                             Notary Public in and for the State of [ADD]

My commission expires on   _____
                                             Date

I hereby accept financial responsibility for any medical treatment for my child by authorizing the use of my medical/hospital insurance.

_____   _____
Type of coverage   Policy number/group number

_____   _____   _____
Company name   Address   City/State/Zip

_____
Name and address of employer

_____   _____   _____
Emergency contact name   Telephone   Relationship

PLEASE ATTACH A PHOTOCOPY OF INSURANCE CARD

Chores Chart

	TUESDAY	WEDNESDAY	THURSDAY	FRIDAY
Breakfast—clean up kitchen				
Breakfast—clean up tables				
Devotions				
Dinner cook				
Dinner cleanup				
Bath cleanup (M)				
Bath cleanup (F)				
Great room cleanup				
Kitchen cleanup				

Sponsor Meeting Before Mission Trip

(I give a copy of this agenda to each sponsor along with a list of participants, copy of travel route, the schedule while on the trip, What to Bring list [Sample 11 in *Resource Section*], and a typical Day-to-Day description [Sample 9 in *Resource Section*])

Reminder: [Sunday, May 23, 11:00 a.m.] service: Commissioning for all going on the trip

DECISIONS REGARDING RENTALS
Vans and U-Haul
- Who will drive church van?
- Who will pick up the rental van (with trailer hitch) and U-Haul trailer (5 x 8')?
  - > Will need to take a church check and chains and locks to the van rental company AND chains and locks. (We use these to chain the U-Haul to a telephone pole or other secure place at the location of accommodations. We need two locks, one for trailer and one for chain.)
  - > Give this volunteer the reservation number for the fifteen-passenger van, along with the location and hours the van rental is open the day before the trip.
  - > Also give this person the reservation number for the U-Haul trailer (5 x 8') along with the location of the U-Haul place and the hours it is open the day before the trip. He/she will likely need to pay with personal credit card; save receipt for reimbursement.
  - > Give this volunteer information regarding the return of the U-Haul and rental van. Instruct them as to whether or not they need to get extra insurance for the rentals. Some church insurance policies cover this and there is no need to purchase it.

DECISIONS REGARDING TRAVEL
- Solicit loaner walkie-talkies if there is to be more than one vehicle.
- Do we let the youth choose in which vehicle they will ride? (Usually we did, though one year the cliques were so obvious, we made van assignments.)
- Give each adult a map of the driving route.
- Decide where you will stop for lunch, especially if the group is large.
- Confirm that adults agree that the youth can use their cell phones/iPhones/iPods while traveling IF they agree to turn them off when we need to give instructions. They will be put away in a box during the week except for a short while at night.

OTHER THINGS TO REVIEW WITH THE SPONSORS USING THE TYPICAL "DAY TO DAY" DESCRIPTION [SAMPLE 9 IN RESOURCE SECTION]:
- Describe what the plan will be upon arrival at the destination. (Eg.: Unload vans and U-Haul; let youth and adults put stuff into their rooms; drive into town to eat dinner and grocery shop).

- If known, describe the communal space for visiting, playing games, devotions. Decide whether there is space for a poster to color, or jig-saw puzzle, or cards.
- Remind the adults, especially those who are not regular sponsors, that all of them have the authority to make a judgment call on inappropriate behavior if necessary, so that issues such as inappropriate language, dress, etc. can be dealt with in a timely manner. They are to remind the youth that they represent our church.
- Everyone needs to pitch in with chores, so there will be a "chores chart" with assignments. (I have found that this kind of chart is not necessary on a trip with college students.) Adults are to be on standby to help supervise if necessary.
- Invite the youth to help out whenever possible: loading and unloading the U-Haul; chaining U-Haul to a tree; carrying coolers, etc.
- Describe meals:
  > Breakfast is normally cereal or bagels and fruit, with coffee. Ask for early riser who is willing to brew coffee.
  > We each make our own lunches and will need to pack them in coolers to take to the job site. The adults can take turns to help supervise this effort.
  > Usual pattern for dinners: each pay for our own supper at a fast food place the night we arrive; dinner the first work day—taco salad; Wed. is usually our day/afternoon off, so local restaurant for supper; on Thursday the Habitat community prepares dinner for us; on Friday (the last night) we order pizza.
  > Leave Saturday about 8:00 a.m. or so. Either finish off the cereal or buy breakfast on the road. The trip money will pay for either.
- Explain affirmation cards.
- Mid-week we write thank-you postcards to "stockholders" who donated money for the trip.
- We have student-led devotions in the mornings; short Bible study in evenings after dinner.
- Who will be responsible for taking photos and shooting video?
- Identify possible activities for the free day or afternoon so that those options can be offered to the youth for their decision
  > Example: When we go to Jonestown, MS to work with Habitat, there are a variety of options: Blues Museum in Clarksdale; drive along the levee and explore downtown Clarksdale; drive to Memphis to tour the Civil Rights museum at the Lorraine Hotel, tour Graceland, see the ducks at the Peabody Hotel at 5:00, eat BBQ at the Rendezvous, etc. Consider money and time as you make decisions.
  > If you plan to show an edited video or slide show of the trip to the congregation later, who will edit and organize the "show"?

CONTACT INFORMATION
- Give each sponsor the contact information for the accommodations, the ministry director with whom you will work, and any other numbers that are important to have.

  > Share one another's cell numbers.

Day-By-Day Schedule MS 2010 *(To be shared with all sponsors)*

Video and photos are taken all week. The video is edited afterwards and/or a digital slide show created for the congregational brunch or lunch.

MONDAY IN VANS

- Pass around clip boards and record sandwich fixings and fruit preferences, then use it to create a grocery list for Monday night. (This grocery list chart is Sample 15 in *Resource Section*). On the grocery list, group items by category: dairy products, produce, cereal and bread, etc. That makes it easy to give a short shopping list to several groupings of teens.

- Headsets, cell phones, iPhones, and other electronic devices are allowed while traveling, but youth will need to set them aside for instructions, decisions. They can use their phones for 30 minutes between dinner and Bible study/worship time or for 30 minutes after the Bible study each evening.

- Take a plastic box to store cell phones.

- Call Rendezvous restaurant in Memphis mid-afternoon for reservations Wed. for 23 people @ 6:00 p.m.—Phone #901-522-8840.

- Call the local Habitat contact person to give him our estimated time of arrival so he can meet us at the convent to let us in and give us a key.

MONDAY EVENING

- After the 10-11 hour drive, get help from youth to unload the U-Haul and van, then chain the U-Haul to a tree or telephone pole.

- Let teens know which rooms are for youth and which for adults; then everyone can haul their own stuff to their designated room. In the case of the convent, guys stayed downstairs, girls upstairs.

- Ask the Habitat contact person if there are any "rules" about the accommodations, such as hot water issues, water pressure issues, rooms/cabinets that are off-limits.

- Check supplies in kitchen facilities to see if basics are there such as sugar, salt, pepper.

- Go into town for dinner at Back Yard Burger (everyone pays for their own).

- Head for the grocery store

- First night: give sections of the shopping list to different groups of youth. As they complete their list, they are to meet the adults at the check-out stand.

- Settle into the convent/volunteer center. Show everyone where towels are, where snacks will be kept, what is available to them in the kitchen, etc.

- Before or after Bible study, go over the expectations with everyone.

- Remind them of the schedule and what they will have to accomplish before departing at 8:15 a.m. for the worksite—15 min. to Jonestown.

- Lights out 11:30 p.m., preferably 11:00.
- Showers in afternoon/early evening—no time in mornings—*short showers*—low water pressure and limited warm water.
- Everyone is to be inside building by dark—can play with Frisbees, etc. outside prior to dark but we are not allowed to let the neighborhood kids into building.
- Who has alarm clocks? And who needs to be woken up?
- Everyone is on their own to fix their own cereal/breakfast and clean up after themselves.
- Everyone makes his or her own lunch each day except Wednesday (sandwiches, packet of chips, packet of cookies, apple or dried fruit packet, napkin and hand-wipe). Put all but the sandwich in a lunch sack with your name on it (Sharpies are in kitchen) and water bottle or Gatorade with your name on it. Put sandwich in baggie with your name on it for the cooler. Before leaving in the a.m., put into vans the two coolers and box w/sack lunches.
- The trip money pays for everyone to have one soda and two snack packs a day. If you want more sodas, etc. for yourself, then you need to buy your own.
- Show them where the Chores Chart (work/clean-up schedule) will be posted.
- Go over the devotions schedule and who is responsible for what.
- Do the Bible study and let them draw names for prayer during the week.

EVERY MORNING IN MS

- Before you have devotions and leave for work site, everyone makes their own breakfast (cereal/fruit/ bagels/yogurt) and lunch:
- Make own sandwich, put it in baggie with name on it marked with Sharpie and then put in jumbo Ziploc bags for double protection from melting ice in the cooler.
- Choose bottle of water or Gatorade to go in cooler—mark name on cap with Sharpie.
- Put apple or other fruit, little bag of chips, little bag of cookies to go in lunch sack with name on it. These sacks are carted to and from the work site in a cardboard box.
- Before leaving for work site, one sponsor needs to take stock of grocery needs for next day or so:
- Ice?
- Bread and sandwich fixings?
- Fruit for cereal?
- Milk, orange juice, and bottled water/Gatorade?

EVERY EVENING IN MS

- During supper everyone shares a funny or memorable moment in their day while sitting around the tables.
- Then let them loose to play or to visit, but as soon as it is dark, gather everyone for the Bible study/worship and sharing time.
- Remember that community building is the focus in the evenings, so as sponsors keep watch for anyone getting left out.
- After the Bible study/worship, we usually play card games in small groups, visit in small groups. Someone can bring Apples to Apples as an alternative. In the past we set out a big poster to color and/or a jigsaw puzzle to work but there is not much table space at the Convent to do that.
- In the afternoon or at least after dinner, remind whoever has the next morning's devotion.
- *At every opportunity look for postcards to send as a "thank you" to Habitat stock holders (it is easier to buy stamps at home) AND at least one evening the kids will want to go to Walmart.*

TUESDAY

- Breakfast, lunch prep, and clean-up of kitchen and eating area.
- Pack drinks and sandwiches into two coolers—one per van—and box with lunch sacks.
- Devotions
- Leave by 8:15 a.m.
- Dinner—Taco salad
- They will ask to go to Walmart, so decide if this is a good night or not. Definitely set a time to meet at the front of the store. No one can hang out alone!
- When gathered for Bible study, pass out Affirmation Cards and explain the purpose of them, especially for the first timers. Remind them what an affirmation card is to do—please put nothing rude, crude, or ugly on them. Try to write a fun memory about each person or something good about each person.
- Remind _____ they have the devotion on Wed.
- Present options for sightseeing and decide on activities for Wednesday afternoon:
  - > The Blues Museum in Clarksdale is famous—good for kids to see the history (postcards are there). Open 9 a.m. to 5 p.m.
  - > Memphis: not enough time to do everything but we have seen the Elvis statue at the visitor's center, toured the Civil Rights Museum at the Lorraine Hotel (order tickets ahead of time—might get discount), watched the ducks at the Peabody Hotel at 5 p.m., walked to Beale Street to see the activities, eaten BBQ at the Rendezvous at 6:00 p.m., in the alley behind South 2nd St.
- Free time

WEDNESDAY—half-day of work

- Devotions
- No need to pack a lunch
- Develop a grocery list
- Leave by 8:15 a.m., work half-day
- Get cleaned up and have lunch at convent
- Buy 52 MS postcards while touring Blues Museum in Clarksdale if they have not been purchased yet
- Memphis: head there by 3:00 p.m. at latest
- Bible study
- Wednesday night, write the Thank You postcards, then mail them the next day. Show the youth where to put address labels, where to write message, where to put stamp as some do not know this! The postcards are to be a thank you to the Habitat stock donors. The youth can either sign their name or just sign "NorthPark youth." Ask youth to mention something about the work they are doing.
- Remind _____ that he/she is responsible for devotions tomorrow.
- Ask: Where do they want the traditional group photo taken: At work site? Convent? Community dinner?
- Free time

THURSDAY

- Group photo today or tomorrow!
- Pack water and Gatorade—two coolers—one per van and box with rest of lunch stuff
- Devotions
- Leave by 8:15 a.m.
- Work
- Dinner with community—probably at the Convent. Our contribution is a large fruit salad
- At the dinner, ask someone who knows the Habitat homeowner about where to get a gift certificate to give to that person on Friday: Walmart? Ace Hardware? (Have given up to $300 in past if it is in the budget).
- Bible Study
- Remind _____ he/she has devotion tomorrow
- Remind everyone about the affirmation cards and the importance of them
- Free time

FRIDAY

- Pack water and Gatorade—two coolers—one per van and box with rest of lunch stuff
- Devotions
- Leave by 8:15 a.m.
- First thing to do on the job site is take a group photo if have not already.
- Dinner: Prepare spaghetti and salad or go out for pizza
- Last Bible study, revealing of prayer recipients (name, what you prayed for them, what you noticed about the person during the week), reflection on the week. Close with circle prayer holding hands.
- Clean up and pack so we can load up first thing Sat. morning.
- Adults decide—breakfast and departure time?
- Free time

RETURN TRIP IN VANS—SATURDAY

- Breakfast
- Load U-Haul and vans
- Give the youth their cell phones
- Leave Convent by 8:00 a.m.
- Pass around clip boards with blank notebook paper so all youth can (anonymously) write down what the trip has meant to them. These comments will be printed in church newsletter.

Orientation Meeting with Youth, Parents, Sponsors

MISSISSIPPI 2010 MISSION TRIP ORIENTATION FOR COLLEGE AND HIGH
SCHOOL PARTICIPANTS AND PARENTS

Have ready a sample "packet" prepared for each family represented that will
include a schedule for the trip, a list of what to bring, any other instructions/
expectations, and a photocopy of the travel route.

NEED

- $150 from each teen /college student
- Habitat waiver for both trips, consent to treat forms (for minors), and
  notarized medical release forms for those whose information is not already
  on file in the youth director's office
- High School parents: check medical insurance info on your teen's notarized
  medical release form for accuracy
- Covenant of Conduct forms from those 18 and under

EXPLAIN TRAVEL PLANS: TWO VANS AND ONE U-HAUL TRAILER

- Long trip—10-11 hours—gather at 6:45 a.m. in the church parking lot
- Travel with walkie-talkies
- We will get tired of one another at some points, so just take a deep breath
  as we can't do anything about it
- Head sets are okay until we ask for attention to announce pit stops, etc.
  Many of the youth and adults play some games between vans, so be alert
  to that so you can participate
- Cell phones/iPhones/electronic devices are okay while we travel but will
  put them in a box during our stay except to make calls after Bible study in
  the evenings for 30 minutes—only to check in with family

GO OVER OTHER INFORMATION AND "TO BRING" LIST

- Put your name on everything
- Describe our accommodations and what is needed: We will be staying in
  a former convent in Clarksdale where there are single twin beds, so bring
  pillow, sheets or sleeping bags. Bring soap; convent provides towels
- Look at the printed travel map in your "packet"—questions about the route?

GO OVER SCHEDULE

- There will be a Chores list posted after we arrive. Everyone is expected to do their share of the work to keep our accommodations clean, so you will be assigned 2-3 tasks to share with a buddy
- We will take off one afternoon and from comments already made by you, we will sightsee in Memphis—61 miles north
- Sunday, June 27 is the mission trip brunch for the congregation. We will need lots of parents/teens to help prepare the food. There is a sign-up sheet being passed around. Please sign up if you will be in town and indicate what you will bring

THE WORK WE WILL BE DOING

- Habitat is trying to get one house finished by end of summer. Two brothers of the recipient will be helping us next week; both are carpenters
- College group will finish siding, pull out insulation and reinstall (was done incorrectly), and level the yard
- High school group will work on dry walling and mudding, completing the porch and fascia board
- (Let the group know the name of the family or group you are helping; ask them to begin praying for the family/group.)
- Habitat furnishes most of the tools needed, but if you have a hammer, pencil, and measuring tape bring them with your name printed clearly on them; NorthPark has nail aprons.
- Just so there is no misunderstanding, we are making a commitment to work. We will have a lot of fun while working, but we are not going just to play and goof off. This is a commitment to serve together those who are in need of our help.

REVIEW THE "TO BRING" LIST (RESOURCE SECTION, SAMPLE 11)

VOLUNTEERS ARE NEEDED TO BRING

- CD Player/radio to play at the convent and at the work site
- Games (such as Apples to Apples) and cards (for Spades or other card games)
- Puzzle—in case we have space
- Two first aid kits
- Two ice chests

- Taco meat—grease drained, mix with taco seasonings, put in baggies, FREEZE. These will be put in the coolers and heated for dinner after our first day of work. For the high school trip we need twelve pounds of meat. We need four people to make three pounds each. (Before orientation, determine how much taco meat you will need according to the numbers in your group. Line up volunteers to cook about three pounds each.)
- Four box fans and four extension cords for the bedrooms

DEVOTIONS

- Ask for youth volunteers for each morning's devotions while on the trip. They can work in pairs but it is helpful to line that up ahead of time in case there is a CD or other item they want to bring as part of the devotion.
- Tuesday
- Wednesday
- Thursday
- Friday

What to Pack List

- Work clothes
  - > Work gloves are a must! Put your name on them
  - > Hammer if you have a favorite, but Habitat has plenty: put name on it!
  - > T-shirts: no tank tops or crop tops with bellies showing!
  - > A long-sleeved shirt in case you are dealing with insulation
  - > Shorts (old ones): not so short we have to view your butt if you are on the roof
  - > Old pants/jeans (for protection)
  - > Sturdy work boots or heavy duty sports shoes
  - > Cap/hat (some work will be in the sun)
- For the twin beds: sheets, pillow, light blanket or sleeping bag
- Washcloth and soap (The Convent supplies towels)
- Casual clothes (for evening activities)
- Pair of shoes in addition to work shoes
- Swimsuit (just in case there is an opportunity to swim)
- Sunscreen and insect repellent
- Toiletries including shampoo and deodorant
- Flashlight
- Alarm clock
- Bible/notebook/personal devotional material
- Robe/cover-up/slippers or something (the bathrooms are down the hall)
- Games/cards
- Water bottle with your name on it! (We'll be drinking lots of water on the job site)

ODDS AND ENDS

- **MONEY:** You will need money for food while traveling (four meals: two lunches, two dinners = about $50-60), and money for any snacks, souvenirs, and WalMart. Everything else will be paid for with money collected from fund-raisers.
- **PACKING:** Space in vans and the trailer will be limited, so please try to cram all of the above into one suitcase plus a sleeping bag or sleeping gear, and one teensy bag for vital necessities in the van. Space in the bedrooms and bathrooms will likely be tight.

Taco Salad Recipe for 28

3–4 bags of Corn Doritos

12 pounds of taco meat (about ⅓–½ pound per person)

2 packages of torn lettuce

8 large tomatoes, chopped

2–3 lbs. of shredded cheddar cheese

2 yellow onions, chopped

4 cans of ranch-style or pinto beans, rinsed off; no need to heat

15 oz. can of sliced black olives, drained

1 ½ lb. tub of sour cream

2 16 oz. jars of Pace's medium picante sauce

Heat the meat. Create an assembly line to build the salad starting with crushed Corn Doritos, then meat, cheese, and the rest in any order.

Pre-Trip Shopping List

(for both high school and college trips—most purchased at SAMs. If you have the space to take these supplies along with you, it will save time and money, as many mission locations do not have discount stores that carry items in bulk.)

- ☐ Cereal (large boxes, not individual servings)
- ☐ 144 plastic bowls
- ☐ 144 plastic spoons
- ☐ 144 10 oz. or 12 oz. paper cups for juice
- ☐ 100 paper/foam plates
- ☐ 100 plastic forks and knives
- ☐ 80 larger paper cups for dinner and other times
- ☐ 1 large package of paper napkins
- ☐ 108 lunch sacks
- ☐ 120 sandwich baggies (Ziploc)
- ☐ Boxes of hand-wipes in individual foil packets
- ☐ 2–3 cases of bottled water (16 oz. size, not huge ones)
- ☐ 2–3 cases of Gatorade
- ☐ 1 case of Coke
- ☐ 1 case of Dr. Pepper
- ☐ 1 case of Lemonade
- ☐ Snack stuff: big jar of pretzels, breakfast bars/snack bars, two to three —other snack foods
- ☐ Boxes with at least 108 little packages of chips
- ☐ Boxes with at least 108 little packages of cookies
- ☐ Boxes with at least 108 little packages of dried fruit (optional)
- ☐ 64 oz.container of Pace's Medium Picante sauce
- ☐ 2 lb. bag of shredded sharp cheddar cheese
- ☐ 52 (number of "stock holders") x 2 (college, high school trips) = 104 postcard stamps (for the thank-you postcards to be sent to Habitat "Stock holders")

Check List of Supplies to Take

- ☐ Affirmation envelopes already labeled with names: one per participant including yourself
- ☐ Devotion/Bible study booklets: one per participant including yourself
- ☐ 2 rolls of masking tape
- ☐ Lots of colored markers
- ☐ 3 pairs of scissors
- ☐ Scotch tape
- ☐ 6 black Sharpies
- ☐ Tax exempt forms
- ☐ Mailing labels for postcards to "Habitat Stock" holders or for donors to your fundraisers
- ☐ Writing pens: enough for each participant to have one
- ☐ 2 clipboards
- ☐ Box for cell phones
- ☐ Legal pad
- ☐ Package of 3 x 5" cards
- ☐ Ziploc sandwich baggies for sandwiches: enough for each day you pack lunches
- ☐ Extra large baggies to put sandwiches in for cooler
- ☐ Lunch sacks: enough for each day you pack lunches
- ☐ Box fans for bedrooms if you are going to a warm place
- ☐ Walkie-talkie for each vehicle
- ☐ Chain, 2 locks and keys for U-Haul
- ☐ Nail aprons, other tools, etc.
- ☐ Kroger/grocery discount card
- ☐ First aid kit for each vehicle
- ☐ Maps?
- ☐ A few large plastic garbage bags
- ☐ Notarized medical release forms
- ☐ Habitat paper work
- ☐ Envelope containing names on strips, for prayer
- ☐ CD player
- ☐ Games
- ☐ 2 decks of playing cards

Preference Chart for Groceries

NAME	CEREAL/YOGURT/ BAGELW	FRUIT	SANDWICH MEAT	CHEESE? MAYO?	SODA TYPE

Basic Grocery List to Purchase Upon Arrival

- ☐ Milk
- ☐ Orange juice
- ☐ Fruit for cereal*
- ☐ Cereals you could not get at SAMs*
- ☐ Bagels, if requested*
- ☐ Coffee
- ☐ Creamer (ask adults if they use it first)
- ☐ Sugar, salt, pepper if not found in kitchen at your facilities
- ☐ Bread for sandwiches
- ☐ 2 loose leaf heads of lettuce for sandwiches
- ☐ 5 tomatoes for sandwiches
- ☐ Sandwich meat and cheese for sandwiches*
- ☐ Mayo, mustard, etc.*
- ☐ Paper towels
- ☐ 2 boxes Kleenex
- ☐ Crackers, peanut butter and dill pickle slices (snack for your group— explanation in Chap. 2)
- ☐ Ice for coolers for lunches
- ☐ Supplies for Taco Salad (for 28)
- ☐ 2 packages pre-torn lettuce for Taco salad
- ☐ 8 tomatoes for Taco salad
- ☐ onions
- ☐ 3–4 bags of Corn Doritos to crunch up
- ☐ 2–3lbs. shredded cheddar cheese (if not already purchased)
- ☐ 1 ½ lbs. sour cream4 cans of ranch style or pinto beans
- ☐ 15 oz. can sliced black olives
- ☐ 2 16 oz. jars of Pace's medium picante sauce
- ☐ Cookies or ice cream sandwiches for dessert on Tuesday night w/ Taco Salad
- ☐ Gallon Ziploc bags for leftovers
- ☐ By Wednesday, find local postcards at grocery store or drug store (# depends upon how many people donated to "Habitat Stock" or other fundraiser)

*Specific brands/types desired come from the Food Preference Chart that was passed around on clip boards during the drive to your location

ACKNOWLEDGMENTS

I t is with profound gratitude that I recognize the community of saints surrounding me in these mission efforts and in the creation of this book. First and foremost, I give thanks for my husband John, who helped with years of garage sale fundraisers by time and again hauling goods to the church in his pickup truck for the sales, and who gave his blessing on my absences due to the trips. (Yes, he probably enjoyed the weeks of peace and quiet!)

I am also grateful to Lynn McIntyre, one of the sponsors on my last trip, who encouraged me to write down my experiences for the benefit of others who plan such trips, and to Lynn, Gary Smith, and Rev. Josh Robinson who helped me in the initial stages of organizing my thoughts. The book would not contain the rich stories it does without the many youth and adults who responded with their reflections....Thank you, thank you! I am indebted as well to my friend and colleague Mary Marcotte for devising the book title, my editor Tom Blackwood, the book designer Elizabeth Fenimore, and Ulrike Guthrie for her final editing and proofing. Each of them helped create what you are reading.

Obviously I would not have had these experiences to write about if it were not for the many youth and adults who made a commitment to partner with me on these trips and who energized and inspired me. Thus, I give thanks to...

Participants from Ridgeview Presbyterian Church, 1988-1993

Laurie Ames (Petty)	Nick Harris	Ryan Parks	Cid Smith
Will Carroll	Mike Hatton	Amy Petrie	Julie Smith
Doug Crane	Rocky Haynes	Leigh Phillips (Norris)	Amy Snead (Jackson)
Gail Darden	Susan Haynes	Paul Ralston	Tiffany Souders
Gary Darden	Carlos Hernandez	Kecia Rezail	Ginny Taylor (Williams)
Jenny Deichler (Gomez)	Jeffrey Hernandez	Bob Roth	Emily Taylor (Magill)
Brooke Dorsey (Mc-	Courtney Keller (Davis)	Dave Saiter	Julie Taylor (Sparks)
Millan)	Lindsey Lafferty	Jonathan Saunders	Roger Taylor
Ben Dismore	Heather LaFontaine	Meagan Schroeder	Charlotte Whitfield
Tom Earthman	Brent Lium	(Brown)	Chris Whitfield
Colin Eft	Jeff Lium	Harold Shuck	Alan Willis
Karen Fitzgerald	Mike Martin	Sybil Shuck	Chris Willis
Ginger Gilchrist	Tom Martin	Wayne Shuck	Judy Willis
David Giles	Jamie Oxley	Whitney Simmons	Jalie Yoe (Watkins)
Glenn Hale	Michael Oxley	(Wilson)	Brent Yost
Ava Harris (Longshore)	Mike Parks	Bob Smith	Mark Young

Participants from NorthPark Presbyterian Church, 1995-2010

Wayne Anderson	Margaret Farris	Logan Lee	Camille Sale
Chanelle Angeny	Melanie Gohn	Rachel Lee	David Schieffer
Seth Archer	Samuel Grant	Michelle Leverett	Sarah Schieffer
Mark Auten	Anthony Gunsalus	Devon Lonergan	Laken Schifelbein
Todd Auten	Gina Gunsalus	Blake Mankin	Emily Siegers
Davis Beard	Brent Hampton	Elizabeth Mauricio	Hannah Siegers
Michael Booth	Chris Hanlon	Lynn McIntire	Cynthia Smith (Carter)
Philip Bredehoeff	Mary Harvey (Easley)	Matthias Meier	Gary Smith
Tyler Briggs	Cherry Haymes	Thomas Meier	Jenny Smith (Raju)
Jessica Brown	David Haymes	Josh (Jake) Miller	Jessica Smith
Sara Buttine	Haley Haymes	Jon Mooney	Kyle Smith
Tom Buttine	Laura Hedrick	Jennifer Moses	Mark Smith
Julia Berry	Lindsey Hedrick	Jennie Nichols	Mimi Smith
Connor Campbell	Emily Herrera	Katie Nichols	Shea Snider
Ian Campbell	Lynn Herrera	Katie North	Veronica Stephens
Andy Cavin	Amanda Herzer	Kim Norvell	Cecelia Stewart (Cox)
Anne Chambers	Ashley Herzer	Brian Nwannunu	Robbie Stewart
Chris Christensen	Martha Herzer	Carl Nwannunu	Katy Stillson
Kristi Click	Siena Hickey	Chijioke Okorie	Kathy Stricker
Reed Click	Jordan Hofeditz	David Orleans	Ryan Strubeck
Stephanie Click (St.	Sara Hofeditz	Joan Orleans	Lorien Swayze
Clair)	Clay Hollingsworth	Kim Orleans	John Swinford
Chad Cooley	Meredith Hollingsworth	Ed Pawkett	Megan Swinford
Steve Cox	Michael Hook	Cheryl Payton	Tyler Temblador
Sam Crow	Simon Hook	J.W. Peters	Adam Waggoner
Kelly Cunningham	Debbie Janasak	Rachel Peters	Jason Waggoner
(Lawrence)	Kara Janasak	Kendra Price	Grant Warner
Kerry Cunningham	Nathan Janasak	Sean Price	Valerie Warner
(Cree)	Cameron Jones	Alyssa Ringhausen	Claire Wilson
Rhia Davis	Damelsa Kaguda	Tori Ringhausen	Olivia Wilson
Tan Do	John Kemper	Josh Robinson	Courtney Zacharias
Nick Doran	Karly Kilroy	Ryan Rodriguez	(Parker)
Braden Fair	Dustin Kindred	Dean Rylander	Donna Zacharias
Mitchell Fair	Jonathan Kocks	Layne Rylander	Jamie Zerwekh
Frank Farris	Will Lawrence	Risa Rylander	

ABOUT THE AUTHOR

Jann with Teola whose Habitat home in Sherard, MS is in the background.

J ann Treadwell is a retired certified Christian educator in the Presbyterian Church (USA). After graduating in 1988 from Perkins School of Theology with a Master of Religious Education, she served at two Presbyterian churches in the Dallas, Texas area over a 22 year period as Director of Christian Education. For six years she was on the denomination's Educator Certification Council and was selected by the Association of Presbyterian Church Educators as their 2010 Educator of the Year. Youth mission trips have been her passion.

She and husband John have two sons, a daughter-in-law and two grandchildren. Older son John C. is an artist living with his wife Yoko in Santa Fe where he owns and operates a recording studio, Frogville Records. John and younger son Brian work together on their two farms in west Texas, raising hay, cows, sheep, and chickens. Brian is dad to our two remarkable grandchildren, Jamie and Allie Kate. Jann and John travel back and forth between Dallas and their farm.